# Natalie Coughlin

## Other books in the People in the News series:

Adele
Maya Angelou
David Beckham
Beyoncé
Justin Bieber
Sandra Bullock
Fidel Castro
Kelly Clarkson
Hillary Clinton
George Clooney
Stephen Colbert
Suzanne Collins
Natalie Coughlin
Miley Cyrus
Ellen Degeneres
Johnny Depp
Eminem
Roger Federer
50 Cent
James Franco
*Glee* Cast and Creators
Jeff Gordon
Tony Hawk
Salma Hayek
Jennifer Hudson
LeBron James
Jay-Z
Wyclef Jean
Derek Jeter
Steve Jobs
Dwayne Johnson
Alicia Keys

Kim Jong Il
Coretta Scott King
Taylor Lautner
Spike Lee
George Lopez
Jennifer Lopez
Eli Manning
Stephenie Meyer
Nicki Minaj
Barack Obama
Michelle Obama
Apolo Anton Ohno
Danica Patrick
Katy Perry
Tyler Perry
Prince Harry
Condoleezza Rice
Rihanna
Alex Rodriguez
Derrick Rose
J.K. Rowling
Shakira
Kelly Slater
Taylor Swift
Justin Timberlake
Usher
Lindsey Vonn
Denzel Washington
Serena Williams
Oprah Winfrey
Mark Zuckerberg

# Natalie Coughlin

WITHDRAWN

By Barbara Sheen

**LUCENT BOOKS**
*A part of Gale, Cengage Learning*

GALE
CENGAGE Learning·

Detroit • New York • San Francisco • New Haven, Conn • Waterville, Maine • London

**Library of Congress Cataloging-in-Publication Data**

Sheen, Barbara.
  Natalie Coughlin / by Barbara Sheen.
     pages cm. -- (People in the news)
  Includes bibliographical references and index.
  ISBN 978-1-4205-0998-4 (hardcover)
  1. Coughlin, Natalie, 1982---Juvenile literature. 2. Swimmers--United
States--Biography--Juvenile literature. 3. Women swimmers--United
States--Biography--Juvenile literature. I. Title.
  GV838.C67S53 2013
    797.2'1092--dc23
    [B]
                                                                    2012044911

Lucent Books
27500 Drake Rd
Farmington Hills MI 48331

ISBN-13: 978-1-4205-0998-4
ISBN-10: 1-4205-0998-5

Printed in the United States of America
1 2 3 4 5 6 7 17 16 15 14 13

# Contents

**Foreword** 6

**Introduction** 8
Pretty Tough

**Chapter 1** 13
"I'm a Water Baby"

**Chapter 2** 26
Making Waves

**Chapter 3** 40
America's Golden Girl

**Chapter 4** 55
International Celebrity

**Chapter 5** 69
A Balanced Life

**Notes** 82

**Important Dates** 88

**For More Information** 90

**Index** 92

**Picture Credits** 96

**About the Author** 96

**F**ame and celebrity are alluring. People are drawn to those who walk in fame's spotlight, whether they are known for great accomplishments or for notorious deeds. The lives of the famous pique public interest and attract attention, perhaps because their experiences seem in some ways so different from, yet in other ways so similar to, our own.

Newspapers, magazines, and television regularly capitalize on this fascination with celebrity by running profiles of famous people. For example, television programs such as *Entertainment Tonight* devote all their programming to stories about entertainment and entertainers. Magazines such as *People* fill their pages with stories of the private lives of famous people. Even newspapers, newsmagazines, and television news frequently delve into the lives of well-known personalities. Despite the number of articles and programs, few provide more than a superficial glimpse at their subjects.

Lucent's People in the News series offers young readers a deeper look into the lives of today's newsmakers, the influences that have shaped them, and the impact they have had in their fields of endeavor and on other people's lives. The subjects of the series hail from many disciplines and walks of life. They include authors, musicians, athletes, political leaders, entertainers, entrepreneurs, and others who have made a mark on modern life and who, in many cases, will continue to do so for years to come.

These biographies are more than factual chronicles. Each book emphasizes the contributions, accomplishments, or deeds that have brought fame or notoriety to the individual and shows how that person has influenced modern life. Authors portray their subjects in a realistic, unsentimental light. For example, Bill Gates—cofounder of the software giant Microsoft—has been instrumental in making personal computers the most vital tool of the modern age. Few dispute his business savvy, his perseverance, or his technical expertise, yet critics say he is ruthless in his dealings with competitors and driven more by his desire to maintain Microsoft's dominance in the computer industry than by an interest in furthering technology.

In these books, young readers will encounter inspiring stories about real people who achieved success despite enormous obstacles. Oprah Winfrey—one of the most powerful, most watched, and wealthiest women in television history—spent the first six years of her life in the care of her grandparents while her unwed mother sought work and a better life elsewhere. Her adolescence was colored by pregnancy at age fourteen, rape, and sexual abuse.

Each author documents and supports his or her work with an array of primary and secondary source quotations taken from diaries, letters, speeches, and interviews. All quotes are footnoted to show readers exactly how and where biographers derive their information and provide guidance for further research. The quotations enliven the text by giving readers eyewitness views of the life and accomplishments of each person covered in the People in the News series.

In addition, each book in the series includes photographs, annotated bibliographies, timelines, and comprehensive indexes. For both the casual reader and the student researcher, the People in the News series offers insight into the lives of today's newsmakers—people who shape the way we live, work, and play in the modern age.

# Pretty Tough

Natalie Coughlin is one of the most talented and successful female swimmers of all time. She has broken many world and U.S. records, including being the first woman in Olympic history to win gold medals in the same event in consecutive Olympics, being the first woman to swim the 100-meter backstroke in under one minute, being the most decorated female athlete in the history of World Championship swimming with eighteen medals, being the most decorated female athlete at the 2004 and 2008 Olympics, and being the first American female to win six medals in one Olympic games. Her speed and ability helped to change perceptions about how fast women can swim, setting the pace for young swimmers, such as Missy Franklin. Coughlin, according to swim coach Jack Bauerle, "has changed swimming. She doesn't break records by the hundredths, she breaks them by body lengths. Thanks to her, what we thought was fast is no longer."[1]

As an Olympian, Coughlin won a medal in every event she entered in three Olympic games, winning five medals at the 2004 Olympics in Athens, Greece; six at the 2008 Olympics in Beijing, China; and one at the 2012 Olympics in London, England. With twelve Olympic medals (three gold, four silver, and five bronze), she is tied with Dara Torres and Jenny Thompson as the most decorated American female Olympian in history.

Moreover, Coughlin is more than a gifted athlete; she is an author, a gourmet cook, an organic gardener, a surfer, a ballroom dancer, a photographer, a philanthropist, a cover girl, and a role model for children. Her athletic prowess, beauty, grace, intelligence, and likeable personality have made her an international celebrity. She has adorned the covers of magazines, been interviewed on television and Internet talk shows, a contestant on *Dancing with the Stars*, a judge on *Iron Chef*, and an Olympic analyst on MSNBC during the 2006 Winter Olympics. A University of California, Berkeley graduate with a bachelor's degree in psychology, Coughlin, according to her long-time coach Teri McKeever, is "a young lady who embodies the whole package."[2]

## Swimming Against the Current

Although Coughlin's talent and natural grace makes everything she does look effortless, her accomplishments have not come easily. In fact, at age six, she was disqualified from her first race.

Since then, she has faced many ups and downs. Injury and illness occurred at the worst times. In 2000 sports analysts predicted that Coughlin, then a teenage swimming sensation, would earn multiple medals at the Olympics in Sydney, Australia. But she injured her shoulder before the Olympic trials and did not make the Olympic team. The injury and the pressure she felt from her tough youth coach made her consider giving up swimming.

In 2003 fate seemed to plot against her again. Coughlin was expected to win seven gold medals at the World Championships, a competition that was considered to be a test run for the 2004 Olympics. She came down with the flu the first day of the meet. Plagued by high fever, she finished twenty-second in the 100-meter backstroke, an event in which she held the world record. She won only one gold medal at the meet. Her disappointing performance caused a stir in the sport's world. Many experts doubted she had the physical and mental stamina to handle the pressure of international competition. Others questioned her commitment. One reporter said that she was a disgrace to her country. As sportswriter Michael Silver explains, "Coughlin was chewed up, spit out and discarded by her sport before she legally earned the right to vote."[3]

## Physically and Mentally Strong

Despite many setbacks, Coughlin repeatedly made swimming history. A good part of her success is due to her competitiveness and her physical and mental strength. She readily admits that she is extremely competitive. She demands a lot of herself and hates to lose. If someone breaks one of her records, she is not satisfied until she breaks their record. And, if she has a bad experience, she takes that experience and learns from it, turning

*Coughlin's competitiveness, physical strength, and mental toughness have been the keys to her success in and out of the pool.*

it into an eventual win. "When I got sick, it was out of my control," Coughlin explains. "To get through that, being ill as I was, made me a stronger athlete."[4]

Part of her being able to turn her bad experiences into wins is her physical and mental toughness. Coughlin can focus her mind and body for hours on end while training. And, she is stubborn and persistent. When she decides to learn something new, she does not give up until she excels. "If she makes her mind up to do something, she will perfect it,"[5] Coughlin's mother insists.

Coughlin explains it this way: "I consider myself pretty tough. Just growing up. . . . I trained five to six hours a day every day, Saturday included, my whole life. I was getting up at 4 a.m. when I was in high school and still going to school, getting good grades. I swam through injuries. . . . More than anything, I think I'm stubborn and so that makes me tough."[6]

## Unique Attributes

Coughlin has to be tough to compete against women who are bigger and stronger than she is. At 5 feet, 8 inches (1.7m) tall, she is shorter, slimmer, and less muscular than most other world-class female swimmers. "I don't think I was supposed to have muscles, because I lose it within a week if I stop working out,"[7] Coughlin admits.

Other physical attributes, however, help Coughlin make up for her size. She has a wingspan (the distance between the tips of the longest fingers when the arms are extended horizontally at the shoulders) of 6 feet, 1 inch (1.9m), which allows her to take fewer and longer strokes than many swimmers, and she is extremely flexible—so flexible that she can bend at the waist and touch her elbows to the floor. This helps her move fluidly through the water without wasting energy. She also has an incredibly powerful kick and is able to stay under water longer than most swimmers. As sportswriter Cynthia Gorney explains,

I've seen spectators shake their head in astonishment while Coughlin is underwater during a backstroke heat, or grab each other and gesture excitedly at the pool. The other racers have popped up already and are swimming hard while the surface of Coughlin's lane remains unbroken. . . . When Coughlin finally appears, first her manicured hands and then the outstretched rest of her, she has almost invariably left her opponents behind.[8]

Clearly, the water has not always been smooth for Coughlin. Yet she is strong enough to face whatever challenges come her way and wise enough to take advantage of her unique abilities. Her dedication, focus, and determination are all part of this tough young woman's life story.

# "I'm a Water Baby"

Natalie Coughlin was born on August 23, 1982, in Vallejo, California, to Zennie and Jim Coughlin. Zennie was a paralegal, and Jim was a police sergeant. Natalie was their first child, and her sister Megan arrived three years after Natalie was born. Neither parent was an elite swimmer. But they enjoyed splashing around in their backyard pool. In fact, Zennie spent many happy days in the pool while she was pregnant. "So," Zennie quips, "Natalie was swimming before she was born."[9]

Held in her parents' arms, Natalie, too, was splashing in the pool only weeks after her birth. "I'm a water baby,"[10] Natalie insists. To ensure the baby's safety, Natalie's parents enrolled her in swimming lessons when she was ten months old.

## Young Competitor

Natalie took to the water like a little fish. When she was six years old, she joined the Benicia Blue Dolphins, a local swim club. She was not yet an outstanding swimmer, but she loved the water and was determined and competitive. As Tuffy Williams, one of Natalie's earliest coaches, recalls,

> I coached her for a year when she first turned eight years old. At the time, there was nothing really spectacular about her. . . . She didn't hold any team records, but as a nine and ten year old she began to make a mark for herself. . . . She was a fun little girl, she was very competitive and came to practice.[11]

Young Natalie was so competitive that she would go full out and not stop swimming until she hit her head on the pool's wall. Indeed, at the time she said that hitting her head was the only thing she disliked about swim meets. The possibility of winning, she admits, was what she liked most. As Natalie explains, "I've been competitive since I was born. . . . It's in my DNA. I love racing and I love pushing myself."[12]

Swim meets were so important to her that the night before a meet she donned her swimsuit, goggles, and swim cap and strutted around the house like a champion. At first, she did not win many races. In fact, she was disqualified from her first race for being too slow. "I entered the 25 fly [25-meter butter-fly]. I couldn't even get my arms out of the water, and I got DQ [disqualified]," she says with a laugh. "I don't know what evil official would DQ a 6-year-old, but it was a little discouraging."[13] As she got older, there were fewer disqualifications and more wins.

## A Full Life

When the Coughlins enrolled Natalie in the Benicia Blue Dolphins, they were not trying to cultivate a world-class athlete. Their only concern was that Natalie was active and having fun. Her father told a reporter,

> People are always asking, "What's Natalie's best time in this?" and I'll say, "I don't know. It's pretty fast." I have friends at work who say, "Don't you know her time is a one-double-oh-whatever?" Her time isn't important. Did she have fun? Did she think she did well? If those are covered, I don't care about the rest.[14]

Natalie's parents wanted her to have a rich full life. So they enrolled her in many activities besides swimming, such as gymnastics, volleyball, ballet, and tap dancing. But water sports were her favorites. Besides swimming, she loved to surf. Her uncle taught her how to surf on the Coughlin family's annual trip to Hawaii. She still is an avid surfer.

*Coughlin's family, including sister Megan, mother Zennie, and father Jim, supported her swimming as well as her other interests as a child.*

During the school year, she attended St. Catherine's Elementary School, a private Catholic school in Concord, California, where the family had moved. She was a straight-A student with many friends. Her former teacher, Mila Evangelista, recalls, "I remember her as a very cheerful, active, friendly girl."[15] On Saturdays, she and Megan, who also joined the Dolphins, went to swim meets. Jim and Zennie, and Zennie's large extended Filipino family, were always in the stands cheering on both girls. On Sundays, the whole family went to church together.

# Proud of Her Roots

Natalie Coughlin is one-quarter Filipino, and she has always been quite proud of her Filipino roots. Her mother is half Filipino, and her grandmother was born in the Philippines. The school that Coughlin attended from kindergarten through eighth grade had a large number of students of Filipino descent, and she has been strongly influenced by Filipino culture. Throughout her childhood, Coughlin was actively involved in the large Filipino community in her hometown of Vallejo, California.

As an adult, Coughlin has been learning Tagalog, the official language of the Philippines. She admits her accent is not good, but she can speak and understand the language. Coughlin has also learned to cook many Filipino dishes. Her grandmother's *lumpias*, Filipino egg rolls, are among her very favorite foods.

Coughlin has many loyal Filipino fans that are very proud of her achievements. She appreciates their support.

## The Terrapins

By the time Natalie was ten years old, her determination and competitiveness began paying off. Even during practice, she made a point of out swimming everyone in the pool. According to her father, "Natalie was always goal oriented. No matter what she did, she had to know everything about it. And when it came to swimming, whatever level she was on, she'd pick out the fastest person around and make a point of saying, 'That's the one I'm going to beat.'"[16]

Natalie did not win every race, but she had promise. "Natalie was the girl who was the first one in the water and the last out," recalls one of her early coaches, Steve Bennett. "She had so much poise and maturity for her age. Her physical and mental skills were head and shoulders above the rest of the kids. Both my wife and I felt that Natalie really had it in her to be a champion. She had potential, but her technique was poor."[17]

With the right training, Natalie might distinguish herself enough to win a college scholarship in the future. With that in mind, Jim and Zennie enrolled her when she was twelve in the Terrapins, a swim club known for producing national event qualifiers who were candidates for swimming scholarships.

The Terrapins' coach, Ray Mitchell, took swimming very seriously. Initially, he was unimpressed with Coughlin. Her technique and form were primitive. He soon realized, however, that what she lacked in skill she made up for in speed, enthusiasm, and determination. Mitchell recalls, "She was sort of a hacker who sprinted from the gun and had little race technique. She would dive in for a 200 [200-meter race], lead by four body lengths at 50 [meters], two body lengths at 100, one body length at 150 and win by an inch. That was not the smartest thing to do, but we saw heart."[18]

Mitchell was a demanding coach. Training was long and rigorous. Practice began at 5 A.M. and ended shortly before school began. It resumed when school ended and lasted until dusk. Natalie thrived. In fact, she usually arrived at the pool so early each morning that she removed the pool cover.

Natalie trained as a middle- and long-distance swimmer in all four competitive strokes—backstroke, freestyle, butterfly, and breaststroke. This type of racing is grueling, but Natalie took to it. "She'd finish a hard set, and as soon as she touched the wall she'd look up at [assistant coach Paul Stafford] with big eyes, like 'OK! What's next?'"[19] Mitchell recalls.

In her first meet with the team, she won three races and got a trophy for single swimmer performance. As her form, technique, and timing improved, she became more and more successful. The better Coughlin got, the harder Mitchell worked her. He frequently had her swim in the fast lane with the strongest boys on the team. Often, she was the youngest and the only girl. She had no problem with this. It was fun to outrace the older boys.

## Making a Splash

By the time Natalie was in high school, she was being named as a possible Olympian in three events for the 2000 games in Sydney. Her achievements were amazing, and accolades were coming at her from many directions. At fifteen years old, she became the first person in history to qualify for all fourteen individual events at the National Championships. "That's what really blew us away," recalls Mitchell. "This kid was getting good at everything."[20]

*Although Coughlin attracted attention as a potential Olympian while still in high school, she was able to make time in her swimming schedule for normal teenage activities.*

At the meet, she missed breaking a world record by 1/100th of a second. *Swimming World* magazine named her the 1998 National High School Swimmer of the Year and put her picture on the magazine's August cover. She made the U.S. National Team, which is made up of the top swimmers in the United States. They train with the goal of representing the United States at elite international competitions, like the Olympics. She also made the Scholastic All-America Team three years in a row and set three high school records at age sixteen. According to Coughlin, "I was really setting myself up for an amazing Olympic trial in 2000. I was kind of the golden child who had so much potential."[21]

At the same time, she was an honor student at Carondelet High School and had many friends both at school and with the Terrapins. She juggled being an elite athlete with hanging out with friends, going to parties and dances, and doing all the normal activities most teenagers do. Although, she went to her junior prom with wet hair because she swam a relay right before the dance. At the time she told a reporter for *Swimming World*,

> I believe swimming is great for giving you the skills you need to do well in school. It teaches you to manage your time effectively and also gives you the discipline you need to get the work done in a timely manner. . . . It gets difficult at times, but friends are very important, and I'm trying not to miss out on a normal teenage life just because I'm a swimmer.[22]

## No Longer a Little Girl

Being both a normal teenager and a world-class athlete was not easy, particularly where Coach Mitchell was concerned. Mitchell prided himself on being tough. And, he was extra hard on Natalie. In an effort to get her ready for the Olympic trials he amped up the pressure, continuously increasing the duration and intensity of her workouts. Coughlin's teammate, Leah Monroe, recalls, "I'd say we all got it pretty bad, but it was different for Nat. She was at a new level Ray [Mitchell] had never dealt with before. Ray's going to put more of himself into his fastest swimmers; he was going to invest as much as he could in her success."[23]

*As a member of the Terrapins, Coughlin worked with a coach who tried to control her actions and decisions both in and out of the pool.*

Coughlin and Mitchell had very different personalities. He lived and breathed swimming, while she needed more balance in her life. Mitchell demanded that Natalie spend every free moment training. He even wanted her to visualize herself racing as she lay in bed at night. Coughlin loved to swim, but she also enjoyed spending time with her friends and family. It seemed to her that the coach was trying to control her life. If anything interfered with training, then he was against it. For instance, he objected to Natalie going with her family on their annual trip to Hawaii. When she went anyway, he faxed a daily training schedule to her that he insisted she follow. At home, he tried to control what she did in her free time. He demanded that she dump her non-swimming friends and give up weekend social activities, which she refused to do. According to Jim, "as Natalie progressed, he wanted to keep control of her. Even as she got older, he treated her like she was 13; he wanted to know where she went in her free time and what time she went to bed."[24]

When Natalie started dating Ethan Hall, a tall, handsome Terrapin swimmer who was three years older than she was, Mitchell tried to break them up, or, at the very least, stop them from seeing each other until after the Olympics. He considered the time that Natalie spent with Ethan an unnecessary distraction and a threat to her focus.

Natalie resented the way the coach was treating her. Although she always had a mind of her own, she was more tolerant of Mitchell's controlling ways when she was younger. Now that she was a young woman, she wanted to be independent and make her own choices, and she disliked the way the coach tried to micromanage her life. Despite Mitchell's best efforts, she did not break up with Ethan.

## Injured

Although Natalie was not always pleased with Mitchell, in the pool she did whatever he told her to do. In 1999, during a particularly tough workout, she felt a sharp pain in her left shoulder. She tried to swim through it, thinking it was just a minor strain.

But the pain only worsened until it became excruciating. She had torn the cartilage around her left shoulder joint, a serious injury especially for a swimmer.

The doctor gave her two choices: surgery to mend the tear or months of painful physical therapy. Because the surgery might permanently limit her range of motion, Natalie chose therapy. But it was not going to be easy.

## The Fun Is Gone

Despite her injury, Natalie kept training. Mitchell insisted she could work through the pain. Most of the time she tried to swim with the injury, but she could barely lift her arm out of the water. Often she trained with a kickboard, doing nothing but leg work. It was not uncommon for her to log 250 laps or about 3 miles (4.8km) a day, just kicking. The workout helped Natalie develop the powerful dolphin kick that she later became famous for. But at the time, swimming with the injury and kicking for miles were torture. Tired, frustrated, and in pain, she found herself

*Coughlin competes in the 200-meter individual medley event at the Olympic trials in 2000. At the time, the pressure of training and the strain of an injury drove her to hate the sport.*

crying as she did lap after lap. When she was not in the water, she was in school or driving back and forth to San Francisco for physical therapy. When she finished a therapy session, she faced a two-hour drive home in rush-hour traffic. Compared to training, which had become so unbearable, she actually preferred the stress of being caught in the traffic snarl. She recalls, "I was so unhappy in practice, I'd much rather sit in traffic. . . . I was just fed up with it. I'd had so much success, and I hurt myself working hard, which is frustrating."[25]

Mitchell was almost as frustrated as Natalie. She was not healing fast enough to suit him. He pressed her to swim despite the pain. He insisted on accompanying her to doctor visits, where he listened to the doctor's recommendations and then came up

# Ethan Hall

There are a number of swim couples in the elite swim world. Swimmers understand each other's training schedule and challenges. Natalie Coughlin married her high school sweetheart, swimmer Ethan Hall, in 2009. Hall was a member of the Terrapins swim club and a skilled breaststroker and individual medley swimmer. He qualified for the Olympic trials in 1996 at age sixteen, and again in 2000, but failed to make the team.

Hall swam at the University of North Carolina at Chapel Hill (UNC) and at the University of California, Santa Barbara (UCSB). He broke UNC's 200-meter breaststroke record in 1999 and had the fastest times in UCSB's 100- and 200-meter breaststrokes. In 2001 Hall was the Big Western Conference 100-meter breaststroke champion.

Like Coughlin, Hall is also well educated. In 2002 he received the UCSB Golden Eagle Award, which is given to the student athlete with the highest great point average.

After graduating from college, Hall became head assistant coach with the Crow County Sea Lions and Shark, youth club swimming teams.

with his own plan for Natalie. As she recalls, "the doctor would say one thing—'You need to rest the shoulder for a month' or 'You're risking future damage'—and Ray would walk out of the room and say I could swim through it. I'd be like, 'What? You were there.'"[26]

Natalie tried to do what Mitchell wanted. But instead of being fun, swimming became drudgery. It hurt, and it was incredibly upsetting. She had lost much of her technique, power, and speed. In the few meets she entered, she finished seconds later than her pre-injury time. In swimming, where races are often won by 1/100th of a second, a few seconds is a very long time.

Mitchell grew increasingly impatient. He kept pushing her. He maintained that her problem was not the injury. Her problem was mental. He berated her from the pool deck as she trained, but his screams did not make her heal faster or swim better. He blamed everything on Natalie's continuing relationship with Ethan. In reality, Ethan, who had been through a number of injuries himself, helped Natalie to cope. "He was really what got me through that horrible year," she explains. "He was someone I could talk to about what I was going through. He'd been through injuries; he knew the environment at Terrapins. Plus he's such a mellow person. He's really goofy and funny and incredibly smart. I definitely would've moved to another club. Because of him I stayed."[27]

By the time the Olympic trials rolled around, Natalie was tired and frustrated with swimming. She felt like she had peaked at sixteen and her swimming career was over. She did not so much dream of going to the Olympics as getting the trials over with. Instead of trying to qualify for three events, she entered only one—the 200-meter individual medley.

Despite all her problems in the water, she qualified for the finals. And, she swam remarkably well in the finals, finishing fourth. That finish, however, did not qualify her for the Olympics, but she did not care. "The whole experience was incredibly trying. I ended up hating swimming," she explains. "I didn't care [about not qualifying for the Olympics]. I wasn't happy. I wasn't upset. I was indifferent. I just thought, 'Well, that's over with.' I just wanted to go to college and have a different environment, a different everything."[28]

Mitchell took Natalie's loss harder. He felt as if Natalie had let him down, and he made his feelings obvious. Natalie then severed her five-year relationship with the Terrapins. She did not know whether she would ever swim again. She started swimming because it was fun. She loved the feel of the water and the thrill of competition. As she got older, her relationship with her coach lessened the fun. Being injured made matters worse. She was discouraged and unhappy. She began to think that devoting herself to swimming was a big mistake.

# Chapter 2

# Making Waves

O nce the Olympic trials were over, Natalie Coughlin wanted to give up swimming. When multiple universities offered her a swimming scholarship, however, she changed her mind. Once she got her degree, she planned to quit the sport for good.

## Parental Conflict

Despite her earlier injury, many universities were eager to sign Coughlin. She preferred to stay in Northern California near her family, which narrowed her choices to Stanford University or the University of California, Berkeley. Coughlin rarely fought with her parents, but when it came to choosing between these two universities, it was war. Both universities are excellent schools. Coughlin's parents preferred Stanford, mainly because it provided on-campus housing for students until they graduated. Berkeley only provided dorm rooms for freshmen. After that, students had to live off campus. Jim and Zennie worried about their daughter living off campus for three years. Zennie was especially concerned about Natalie having to cook her own meals. That particular worry turned out to be ironic since Coughlin would later become a gourmet cook.

Coughlin preferred Berkeley for a number of reasons. It was known for its progressiveness, liberal atmosphere, and diverse student body, which attracted her. She also liked the urban campus and the surrounding community. Stanford was more conservative and traditional. Berkeley seemed better suited to Coughlin's free-thinking, independent nature.

# The University of California, Berkeley

The University of California, Berkeley is part of California's public college system. Established in 1868, it is one of the most highly rated universities in the world. The 160-acre (65ha) campus is located on the eastern shore of San Francisco Bay. The university has always attracted freethinkers and activists who challenge traditional ideas about society, learning, culture, politics, and science. In the 1960s and 1970s, Berkeley students spearheaded many movements, including those for free speech, civil rights, disability rights, and women's rights; and they were at the forefront of the protests against the Vietnam War.

Among other great achievements, Berkeley scholars have won Pulitzer and Nobel Prizes, discovered vitamins E and K, formulated a mixture of helium and oxygen for deep-sea diving, invented the first wet suit, developed the flu vaccine, discovered cancer-causing oncogenes, founded the first biotech company in the world, identified cancer-causing agents known as carcinogens, produced the first microscopic motors, developed new biofuels, and enlisted more than three thousand Peace Corps volunteers.

The university enrolls a total of about thirty-six thousand graduate and undergraduate students. Most were at the top of their high school graduating classes. Seventy-three percent come from California. The university offers more than seven thousand courses and 130 academic departments.

Coughlin also differed with her parents about which school better fit her needs as a swimmer. Stanford was the number-one swimming school in the country. Most swimmers jumped at the chance to be a member of its team. Stanford's coach, Richard Quick, was one of the most acclaimed coaches in the country. He had been the head coach for the 2000 women's Olympic swim team, which was the third time he had that honor. He had coached Olympic medal-

*Coughlin, posing in her University of California, Berkeley swimsuit and cap, clashed with her parents over her decision to attend the school.*

ists Summer Sanders, Jenny Thompson, and Coughlin's childhood hero, Janet Evans. It was an honor to train under him. Jim and Zennie liked Quick. So did Coughlin, but not enough to want to swim for him for the next four years. She knew Quick would push her to be the best swimmer she could be, but after Coach Mitchell, she was wary of being pushed too hard.

Berkeley's coach, Teri McKeever, was different. First, she was a woman, and Coughlin liked the idea of a female coach. Unlike Mitchell, McKeever was easygoing, and she welcomed her team members' opinions and feedback. Coughlin was immediately drawn to her. Her parents felt differently. It was not that they disliked McKeever; in fact, they would become extremely close to her in the future. When they first met her, however, they hardly got a chance to get to know her. During their first meeting, Mike Walker, McKeever's assistant coach, dominated the conversation. He cut McKeever off when she tried to speak and acted like he was in charge. Jim and Zennie found him overbearing. They did not want him working with their daughter. McKeever was going through some personal problems at the time, and her self-esteem was low. She let Walker take advantage of her. But when she learned that Coughlin's parents were against their daughter going to Berkeley because of Walker, she fired him. Even if Coughlin selected Stanford, McKeever realized it was time for her to take charge.

Coughlin, too, took charge. Despite her parents' misgivings, she signed a letter of intent, accepting a place at Berkeley.

## A Good Match

Coughlin's instincts were spot on. She loved Berkeley, and McKeever turned out to be just the coach she needed. When it came to dealing with the young women on her team, McKeever considered the whole person, not just the swimmer. She really cared about the team members, treating them like her own family. As she explains,

> the team is an extension of your family because you spend a lot of time together. You see the best and worst of one another.

*In contrast to the tough style of coaching she endured as a member of the Terrapins, Coughlin thrived under the direction of Berkeley swim coach Teri McKeever, right.*

You also have tremendous experiences together that help you learn about different people and respect them for what they add to the team. A successful team appreciates each individual's contributions and lets each individual be their best. A good team challenges and supports one another too.[29]

That philosophy resonated with Coughlin, especially after her experiences with Mitchell.

Coughlin also liked the fact that McKeever did not believe athletes should train through pain. When Coughlin looked exhausted, McKeever shooed her out of the pool and encouraged her to go surfing or visit Ethan Hall at the University of California, Santa

Barbara, for a few days. "It's all about having a happy, healthy person, not a happy, healthy swimmer,"[30] McKeever says.

# A Wounded Animal

It was obvious to McKeever that Coughlin was not a happy, healthy swimmer. Her attempt to train while she was injured had caused her to become seriously out of balance. One side of her upper body was strong and athletic, while the other was weak and misshapen. Coughlin needed to change her stroke in order to strengthen her weak side. This would help reshape her body and protect her shoulder from further injury. It would also make it easier and more pleasurable for Coughlin to race.

McKeever called in Oregon-based, swim-stroke coach Mike Nelms to help. According to Nelms, watching Coughlin swim was

> like a coyote that's chewed its leg off in a trap. When you have a trauma like that, your nervous system creates movement patterns to avoid utilizing what's hurt. It was like she was bucking on one side, and maintaining her movement on the other—like jamming a skateboard forward on one side and coasting on the other.[31]

Because she was struggling, Coughlin was open to adopting whatever changes McKeever and Nelms came up with. She explains,

> The biggest thing was that I was in such a place mentally when I came to [Berkeley] that I didn't really care how my swimming career turned out at that point. Teri . . . presented me with all those stroke changes, and if I had been healthy and swimming well, I would have been stubborn. But because I was injured, I listened and I improved. I was in the right place at the right time. I think that extended my career. The stars aligned for me on swimming at that time.[32]

Most swimmers would have had difficulties changing their stroke. But making the changes came easily to Coughlin. She was a really fast learner with a remarkable ability to absorb suggestions and immediately incorporate them into her swimming. According to Coughlin, this ability is "almost like OCD [obsessive-compulsive disorder]. I can focus on my whole body for . . . hours, just constantly going up and down and evaluating what is going on."[33]

## Having Fun Again

The changes McKeever and Nelms made to Coughlin's stroke took stress off her shoulder. As a result, she could swim more efficiently and with more ease. And, the coach's quirky untraditional training methods made swimming fun again. McKeever believed that proper technique, body awareness, flexibility, balance, and body positioning were more important than yardage and the intensity of training. And, she wanted training to be fun. So, in addition to swimming, she had her team dancing, practicing yoga and Pilates, riding bicycles, running, lifting weights, and kickboxing. These activities increased the team members' strength, flexibility, and body awareness, while relieving the monotony of routine training.

*As a member of the Berkeley swim team, Coughlin regained her love of swimming.*

McKeever liked to mix things up in the pool, too. She came up with games, silly competitions, and experimental training activities, like underwater wrestling matches, that made swim practice fun. McKeever says,

> As a coach my job is to keep the training exciting and relevant to the athlete's racing experiences. That way the athlete will want to train because they know that their hard work will help them come race time. Different things definitely motivate different swimmers. I think being a good coach is figuring out how best to motivate each individual and the team collectively. Sometimes it's just a matter of trial and error and asking the right questions and being a good listener.[34]

At the time, McKeever's training methods were laughed at by swimming traditionalists. Such methods, they predicted, would fail to produce world-class swimmers. But Coughlin proved them wrong. McKeever's methods were tailored to Coughlin. Within a few months, Coughlin was once again having fun in the pool. She told a reporter,

> I didn't have many expectations when I started college. College and college swimming is a wonderful experience. . . . Swimming is a sport, so it is something you should enjoy. Since we're working out so many hours a week, you might as well give it your best and enjoy every minute. Because if you're not using every minute to your advantage, you're wasting time. And, if you're not enjoying it, you're wasting time. I don't think I ever liked swimming more than I do now. I always thought as soon as college was over, I'd quit swimming, as soon as my eligibility was up I'd quit. The last few months I started thinking I should do this as long as I can, as long as I am enjoying it.[35]

# College Life

Coughlin was also enjoying college life. She had always been a good student, who took her studies seriously. Interested in people and the human mind, she majored in psychology. Despite the hours she spent training and competing, she still maintained a 3.5 grade point average. She enjoyed the camaraderie of being part of a collegiate team and made lots of friends at Berkeley, both on the team and off. Coughlin was especially close to her teammate and training partner, Haley Cope. One summer, the two took a twelve-week cooking class together. Learning to cook was important to Coughlin. In her sophomore year she moved into a studio apartment off campus, where she had to prepare her own meals. Coughlin dove into cooking with the same intensity with which she trained and studied. Once a week, she went home and had dinner with her family. She learned to prepare many Filipino specialties by watching her mother on these visits. She also poured over cookbooks and watched cooking shows on television. As she explains, "I hated the dorm food so much that I couldn't wait to get my own apartment and cook for myself. At first, I could only make crepes, but I started watching cooking shows, reading magazines, and practicing. . . . [Now] I wind down in the kitchen."[36]

It was not long before cooking became her favorite hobby. On Saturdays, she and her sister, Megan, pursued another hobby—shopping. The sisters were good friends and had a lot of fun hanging out together, while shopping for the latest fashions.

On the dating scene, Coughlin continued her relationship with Hall. When he graduated from college, he moved in with her. Despite her busy schedule, Coughlin maintained an active social life, although she often left gatherings early in order to get up at 5 A.M. to train. In 2002 she told a reporter,

> The team is in the water at 5:45 and we work out for two hours. Then, we work out again for at least three hours in the afternoon—swimming, running, yoga, weights. And we have no off-season in this sport. There are always meets, never a time of year when you can just do conditioning. One whole week without training is huge. . . . You can't back off from the 30 hours a week this takes."[37]

Yet, Coughlin did not see herself as being especially disciplined. She had always been good at balancing the various aspects of her life successfully.

# World Champion

Coughlin's renewed dedication to swimming combined with her improved technique, made her a threat at swim meets. She switched her events from long distance to sprints, which were easier on her shoulder and lots of fun. It was not long before she was once again tearing up the waterways. In fact, she only lost one race in her entire collegiate swim career.

Coughlin did not simply win races; she shattered one record after another. In her first two years at Berkeley, she set four world records; broke collegiate records in the backstroke and the butterfly; won five national titles at one meet, becoming the first swimmer since Tracy Caulkins in 1978 to ever do so; and was named the NCAA (National Collegiate Athletic Association) swimmer of the year. By the end of her junior year, she had won every national honor possible in U.S. swimming, some more than once. By her senior year, she held seventeen

*During her career at Berkeley, Coughlin set several world and collegiate records and won multiple national titles—achievements that earned her many honors in the swimming world.*

# Swimming Terminology

The sport of swimming has a language all its own. Here are some common swimming terms.

**anchor:** The final swimmer in a relay.

**blocks:** The starting platforms, located in front of each swim lane.

**club teams:** Year-round swim teams that are organized by age.

**competitive strokes:** The breaststroke, butterfly (fly), backstroke, and freestyle (free).

**dolphin kick:** A kick in which both legs kick in time together.

**event:** A swim race.

**individual medley (IM):** A swimming event in which a swimmer uses each of the four competitive strokes for a specified length of the race.

**kickboard:** A flat float that swimmers hold in front of them as they perform kicking drills.

**lane:** A specific area of a swimming pool designated by ropes; pools are divided into lanes, similar to lanes in a freeway, so swimmers can race and practice in straight lines from one end of the pool to the other without crashing into other swimmers.

**lap:** The distance from one end of a swimming pool to the other.

**leg:** The part of a relay that is swum by an individual swimmer.

**meet:** A complete series of swim events.

**prelims (preliminaries):** Races in which swimmers qualify for the finals; also called heats and semifinals.

**qualifying time:** The amount of time in which a swimmer needs to complete an event in order to enter a swim meet.

U.S. records, five world records, and six NCAA records. And, she was the first woman in the world to swim the 100-meter backstroke in under one minute. Not only that, just to prove to herself and the world that she could still swim long distances, in 2002 she entered a 500-meter, free-style race. Her time was the fifth fastest in history. To honor her achievements, USA Swimming, the national governing body for swimming in the United States, named her the 2002 Swimmer of the Year, the NCAA named her Swimmer of the Year three times, and *Sports Illustrated* magazine named her the 2004 Female on Campus Athlete of the Year.

Many experts were calling Coughlin the greatest collegiate swimmer of all time. In a *Sports Illustrated* article spotlighting Coughlin, swimmer, sports analyst, and 1984 Olympic gold medalist Rowdy Gaines, said of Coughlin: "I haven't seen any-one else like her, not even [five-time Australian Olympic gold medal swimmer] Ian Thorpe. Put her in any event, and she might win it."[38]

Coughlin was also distinguishing herself on dry land. She was becoming a spokesperson for the University of California, Berkeley and for the team. Her pleasant demeanor, all-American good looks, and megawatt smile were making her a favorite with the media. She appeared on the television show *Today* as a celebrity chef. There, she displayed her charm and newly developed cooking skills as she chatted and prepared a pork tenderloin and risotto with host Al Roker. Her performance was a big hit with the media and with the American public who welcomed her into their hearts.

## A Major Decision

Despite all the swimming records and the accolades, Coughlin was not yet a professional athlete. In 2003, at the start of her senior year, she had a chance to change that. She was eligible to become a professional swimmer. Doing so would allow her to accept lucrative sponsorship deals that would make her a rich young woman. Turning pro would also put her further in

*Coughlin cheers after Berkeley's win over rival Stanford in a dual meet in February 2002. Coughlin delayed going pro to compete in the meet, which was Berkeley's first victory over Stanford in nearly thirty years.*

the spotlight, which could lead to all kinds of other interesting opportunities.

On the down side, however, she could no longer be on the Berkeley swim team, even though she could still train with McKeever. This meant she could no longer participate in collegiate meets. There was still one meet that she really wanted to compete in. It was a dual meet between Berkeley and Stanford, traditional rivals. Berkeley had not won the event in twenty-eight years; but the team had come close to winning the last three years. Coughlin wanted one more chance to beat Stanford and take home a win as a thank-you gift for McKeever, who had helped turned Coughlin's life around. It meant so much to Coughlin that she decided to wait to turn pro until March of her senior year, when all her collegiate events would be finished.

The meet, which included diving and swimming, was a nail-biter. Stanford's dive team was far superior to Berkeley's. The swim team had to make up a lot of points to defeat their rival. With only two events left, Stanford needed only eleven points to win. It did not look good for Berkeley. Coughlin acted like a crazed cheerleader, pushing her teammates on. But it was her performance in the 100-meter backstroke that helped spur Berkeley to victory. Coughlin broke the NCAA record and missed breaking the U.S. record by 0.05 seconds. For the first time in almost three decades, Berkeley was victorious. Coughlin and the rest of the team were elated to bring home a win for McKeever. The win was proof to the rest of the swimming world that the coach's unconventional training methods and her de-emphasis on yardage were effective. The win also helped Coughlin prove to her parents that her choice of Berkeley over swimming powerhouse Stanford four long years ago had been the right one.

Indeed, going to the Berkeley was the best decision Coughlin had ever made. She loved the university, her studies, and collegiate life. And, under the guidance of McKeever, she had become one of the best collegiate swimmers in history. Most importantly, Coughlin loved swimming again.

# Chapter 3

# America's Golden Girl

With college graduation and the 2004 Olympics in Athens approaching, Coughlin was under a lot of pressure. Whether or not she could deal with the pressure and succeed in Athens remained to be seen.

## Failure in Barcelona

Berkeley's victory against Stanford was one of the high points of Coughlin's senior year. However, she began her senior year on a low note. In July 2003 Coughlin, accompanied by her family and coach, went to Barcelona, Spain, to compete in the weeklong World Championships. Coughlin was scheduled to swim in seven events, the most of any American. She was expected to win a gold medal in each one. The meet was the last international competition before the 2004 Olympics. The outcome of the meet was considered a predictor of what would happen in Athens.

On the first day of the meet, Coughlin came down with a bad virus that gave her a high fever, chills, a headache, a sore throat, and body aches and pains. Despite her illness, on day one she managed to swim her leg of the 4 x 100 freestyle relay well enough to propel the U.S. team to victory. But the swim took so much out of her that, later that day, Coughlin, the world record holder in the 100-meter backstroke, failed to qualify for the finals in that race.

*Coughlin, third from the top, competes in a heat of the 100-meter backstroke event at the World Championships in Barcelona, Spain, in July 2003. Weakened by a virus, she failed to qualify for the finals even though she was the world record holder.*

It was the biggest story of the meet, and rumors spread like wildfire. Had Coughlin lost her edge? Had she folded under the pressure? Was this a repeat of the 2000 Olympic trials? A very sick Coughlin met with the press to quell the rumors. She admitted she had a fever but did not go into detail. That same night, feeling even worse, she swam in the 100-meter butterfly finals. She tried to go out fast and see how long she could keep up the pace. Despite a good start, her body would not cooperate. Early on, her muscles filled with lactic acid and burnt terribly. Wracked with pain, she forced herself to finish the race. Although she had given her all in the race, she came in dead last. When she was asked why she decided to swim that race, she said that she felt it was cowardly to drop out of the competition. And, although the rest of the world did not see it that way, she felt she accomplished something simply by participating. As she explains, "I was really proud of myself for sucking it up and swimming through my sickness. Everyone thought the meet was a disaster for me and that I should be devastated, but it actually ended on a redeeming note."[39] Yet, after what happened in Barcelona, some in the swimming community questioned whether she had what it takes to be an Olympian.

## Under Pressure

Coughlin's performance at the World Championships put her under pressure to train harder in order to prove to the world that she was still a champion. But her health did not cooperate. For months after Barcelona, Coughlin, who was usually quite healthy, suffered from a variety of colds and viruses that made it impossible for her to train at peak intensity. It did not help that she had to train for both collegiate events and for the Olympics. Collegiate events are held in a 25-meter pool, or short course, and Olympic events are held in a 50-meter pool, or long course. Every training lap Coughlin swam had to be viewed from two perspectives. The two courses required different techniques and racing methods. Essentially, she faced double the training load.

Coughlin was also feeling pressure from her college teammates. Even though she had given up a lot to remain a member

*While at Berkeley, Coughlin was often criticized by other members of the swim team who resented the special treatment she received from the coaches and the media's focus on her achievements.*

of the team rather than turn professional, her teammates took her achievements and contributions for granted. They resented the special treatment she seemed to be receiving from McKeever, how her training differed from theirs, how she sometimes missed team practices to focus on Olympic training, how she always got to swim in the best lane, and how she was singled out by the media, among other things.

Although nothing was said to her face, Coughlin was aware of the tension, the whispering behind her back, and the coolness of her teammates. Nor did she have the support of her training partner and close friend, Haley Cope. Cope, who was also training for the Olympics and understood the kind of pressure Coughlin was under, had transferred to the University of California, Davis.

In January 2004, when the team went to training camp in Australia, Coughlin's isolation from her teammates increased, as did their resentment toward her. Much of the time, instead of training with the team, Coughlin was in a separate pool working with McKeever and Nelms to improve her form in preparation for the Olympic trials. Many of her teammates viewed this as preferential treatment. And, when the team went shopping and sightseeing, Coughlin stayed behind—not because she did not want to participate, as some of her teammates thought, but because she had to train. According to her teammate Marcelle Miller, "no one was talking about it in front of Natalie, but everyone was thinking it. They were all mad at her. We had a bad team attitude."[40]

Finally, McKeever called a team meeting in which she defended Coughlin and reminded the team about how much Coughlin had done for them. In fact, the trip to Australia never would have happened if it was not for Coughlin, who agreed to make a number of celebrity appearances in Australia in exchange for help with the team's expenses. "You guys need to stop worrying about what Natalie's doing and focus on yourselves," McKeever advised the team. "She might not be doing what you're doing, but trust me, she's preparing the way she needs to prepare."[41] Coughlin cried as the coach spoke. The lecture did not completely resolve the situation, but it did clear the air and relieve some of the pressure Coughlin faced from her peers.

# Many Changes

At the same time, Coughlin was dealing with other major changes in her life. She bought a condo in Emeryville, California, which she paid for with the medal money she earned at certain elite swimming competitions. NCAA and USA Swimming regulations allowed amateur athletes to keep this money. Although she loved her new home, it was farther away from campus than her former apartment. She could no longer go home whenever she had a break during classes or training, which disrupted the schedule she had kept for the last three years. When she was home, she spent a lot of time decorating. Always a perfectionist, she wanted everything to look a certain way.

In school she was taking her heaviest and most challenging course load. Coughlin was not the type of student who could settle for mediocre grades, so she was putting in even more hours than usual on her studies.

She was also being pursued by a number of sports agents who wanted to represent her when she became a professional athlete in March. Choosing an agent was an important decision. Coughlin's agent would be responsible for advising her on business matters, marketing Coughlin to sponsors, negotiating contracts for product endorsements, and handling Coughlin's public image. Coughlin had to meet with each prospective agent in order to make an informed choice. Whomever she selected had to be someone she liked, trusted, and could work with. Just as Coughlin had wanted to avoid an overly controlling coach when she chose a college, she also wanted to avoid an overly controlling agent. From the start, Coughlin insisted on being involved in shaping her public image and carefully selecting the products she would endorse. Coughlin refused to endorse any product she did not like or to be marketed as a sex symbol. Whomever she selected as her agent had to be willing to accept Coughlin's involvement. Among the possibilities was the Octagon Agency, which had just signed swimmer Michael Phelps. To woo her, that agency arranged for Coughlin to throw out the opening pitch at an Oakland A's game. That was fun. But Octagon was a large traditional agency, which Coughlin did not feel was a good match for her. In the end,

*Coughlin, looking to expand her public image as a professional, throws the ceremonial first pitch at an Oakland A's game in 2003.*

just as Coughlin selected McKeever and Berkeley over traditional Stanford, she selected Janey Miller, a sports agent who was starting her own company. Miller was the first agent who seemed to genuinely want to collaborate with Coughlin, rather than lead the relationship. Coughlin liked that about her, and she liked the idea of working with a female sports agent. Once again, Coughlin

# Swimming Trivia and Fun Facts

- With nineteen medals, American swimmer, Michael Phelps, is the most decorated Olympian in history.
- American swimmer, Johnny Weissmuller was the first person to swim the 100-meter freestyle in under a minute. He went on to play Tarzan in the movies.
- Elephants can swim up to 20 miles (187km) a day. They use their trunks as snorkels.
- The first swim goggles were made of polished, clear tortoise shell.
- The first recorded swimming races were held in 36 B.C. in Japan.
- The *Titanic* was the first ship to have a swimming pool.
- An estimated sixty-five thousand Americans do not know how to swim.
- American swimmer Steve Genter won a silver and bronze medal in the 1972 Olympics while swimming with a collapsed lung.
- Swim fins were invented by Benjamin Franklin.
- Kangaroos are excellent swimmers.
- An hour of vigorous swimming burns up 650 calories, more than bicycling or walking.
- Swimming works all the major muscles and strengthens the heart and lungs.
- The breaststroke is the slowest Olympic swim stroke. Freestyle is the fastest.

made a decision based on instinct, and she was right. Miller and Coughlin turned out to be a good match.

Once Coughlin's collegiate swimming career officially ended, one of the first deals Miller made was with Speedo, the swimwear manufacturer. Both Speedo and sportswear manufacturer, Nike, wanted to sponsor Coughlin. Since the companies are competitors, Coughlin had to choose between them. Both companies offered her a large sum of money in exchange for Coughlin promising to use their products and make personal appearances for the company. Coughlin liked both company's products. She wound up choosing Speedo. In an effort to share their new technology, Speedo gave world class swimmers their newest products to try without charge. Coughlin appreciated this. In addition, Speedo promised to contribute 5 percent of any bonus money Coughlin earned to Berkeley's women's swimming program. Although swimmers are not paid to compete in the Olympics, they do receive monetary bonuses from their sponsors for winning medals and setting world records. This was very important to Coughlin. Even though she was now a professional athlete, she did not forget where she came from.

## Breaking the Streak

Despite all that was going on in her life, Coughlin managed to get through her final year of collegiate swimming with grace. Up to her final collegiate event, she had never lost a collegiate race. Coughlin won twelve NCAA titles with Berkeley's swim team, the second-most titles for any collegiate woman swimmer in NCAA history. Although this was something to be proud of, her winning streak weighed heavily upon her. She did not know how she or the swimming world would react if she lost a race.

Her final collegiate meet was the NCAA championship. In that meet she handily defended her title in the 100-meter backstroke and butterfly and spurred her team to a stunning victory in the 4 x 200-meter freestyle relay. Coughlin swam the first leg of the race in an incredibly fast 1:55.82 minutes. Her time gave Berkeley a huge lead, allowing the team to win a gold medal and smash the NCAA record for the event. Coughlin's final race, the last of her collegiate career, was the 200-meter backstroke, an event she disliked. Tired from her previous races, Coughlin did not pace herself well. She came out too quickly on her first lap then felt herself fading fast. Her muscles started burning and she had to slow down. For the first time in her college career, she did not win a race. She came in third, but felt no remorse. Oddly enough, she was relieved.

*Coughlin poses for the media at an event to promote the U.S. Olympic swim team in July 2004.*

The pressure of keeping up her winning streak had taken away a lot of the joy of swimming. Now that she lost a race, she realized that the experience was not as bad as she expected. She was ready to move on, turn professional, and go back to racing for the challenge, which was what she loved.

## Professional Athlete

Once the meet ended, so did Coughlin's collegiate swimming career. She was now a professional athlete. To celebrate, she temporarily dyed her blonde hair brown and bought herself a brand-new car. And, she resumed training with McKeever. The difference was now she could concentrate solely on the Olympics, which gave her training more focus and made Coughlin's life a little easier.

Going into the Olympic trials she qualified to swim in four individual races. If she did so and qualified for the Olympics

*Coughlin celebrates her victory in the 100-meter back-stroke final with second-place finisher Haley Cope, right, at the Olympic trials in July 2004.*

in each individual race, she would also be qualified to swim in three Olympic relays—a total of seven events. Swimming in seven Olympic events requires almost superhuman strength and stamina. Between the preliminary races, semifinals, and finals, Coughlin would be swimming about twenty times, often with only minutes between races. There were also press conferences and sponsorship activities to contend with. It did not make sense to attempt this kind of schedule. Coughlin decided she would swim in only two individual events at the trials. If she qualified for these, she would also qualify to swim in three relays. Such a schedule would be hard enough. As she told reporters, "it's keeping my first Games a lot more manageable for me, mentally. I don't want to have too much on my plate. . . . This isn't a meet where you do your swim, you warm down and then you do your next swim. You have to do press conferences, you have to do drug testing. It's very exhausting."[42]

So, before going into the Olympic trials, Coughlin had to decide which two events she would enter. It was a given that she would swim in her world record–holding event, the 100-meter backstroke. Because of the timing of the races, she dropped the 100-meter butterfly. This left the possibility of entering the 200-meter backstroke or the 100-meter freestyle. Of the two, the 200-meter backstroke was her best chance for a gold medal. The other competitors were not as strong in the event as Coughlin. The 100-meter freestyle, on the other hand, had many exceptional swimmers competing in it. It was possible Coughlin would be beaten out of an Olympic spot at the trials. And, even if she did qualify for the event, the international competition was even tougher. World record holder Inge de Bruijn would be representing the Netherlands, and both of the Australian swimmers were very fast. For ultracompetitive Coughlin, measuring herself against the best was what it was all about. So, she chose the 100-meter freestyle rather than the less-challenging, 200-meter backstroke. "It's a tougher path, but I embrace it. And if I win that gold medal, it'll really mean something,"[43] she explains.

Coughlin met the challenges she set for herself at the Olympic trials. Only two swimmers in each event qualify for the Olympics. Coughlin had to come in first or second in the 100-meter backstroke and in the 100-meter freestyle to qualify for the team. She won the 100-meter backstroke, setting the third fastest time in swimming history. Making her victory even sweeter, the second place finisher was her good friend, Haley Cope. The 100-meter freestyle was a closer race. Coughlin came in second, which qualified her for the Olympics.

Coughlin was ecstatic with her performance at the trials. As she stepped on the medal stand, she danced around, punching the air like a champion boxer. Her parents, sister, grandmother, aunts, Hall, and McKeever all cheered her on from the stands, as did most of the swim community who knew about all the struggles she had endured. It was now official. Coughlin was an Olympian. And, because of Coughlin's importance to the Olympic team, McKeever was named assistant coach of the women's Olympic swim team.

# History of the Olympics

**A**thletes have been competing in the Olympics since 776 B.C. The first Olympics was held in Athens. Greece. It featured only one sport—a 192-meter run. Thereafter, the Olympics was held every four years until A.D. 393. By that time, chariot racing, boxing, horse racing, and marathon running had been added to the events.

The next Olympics did not occur until 1896. Once again, it was held in Athens. Three hundred athletes from 13 countries competed. In comparison, 10,500 athletes from 205 countries participated in the 2012 Olympics in London.

Women first competed in the Olympics in 1900. There were 19 women out of 907 athletes competing in five sports—croquet, tennis, sailing, golf, and horseback riding. By the 2012 games, 40 percent of the athletes were women.

The Winter Olympics, which features cold-weather sports, such as skiing, ice-skating, and bobsledding, began in 1924. It is held two years apart from the Summer Olympics. The logo for both the Winter and Summer Olympics is five linked gold rings. Each ring symbolizes one of the five continents from which the athletes come.

## America's Best

Coughlin's new professional status combined with her stellar performance at the Olympic trials put her in the public eye. Sportscasters were calling her America's Golden Girl. In one day alone, she did ten hours of interviews and photo sessions. She got to test her acting ability in a movielike commercial for NBC, promoting the upcoming Olympics. But even with her busy schedule, her first priority was training. As she told a reporter,

> I've been able to do a lot of cool things in the past few weeks. The NBC coverage for the Olympics has been really fun. I worked on my acting skills. I shot an extended commercial. It was fun. I got to work with a green screen, which they superim-

posed action of people on the screen. It was interesting talking to people who weren't there. I'm able to enjoy these things but it's not taking away from my training. . . . I don't think you can be too prepared. I definitely feel prepared and ready to go.[44]

## Olympic Champion

Coughlin was prepared. She medaled in every event she entered, winning a gold medal in the 100-meter backstroke and in the 4 x 200-meter backstroke relay, a silver medal in the 4 x 100

*Coughlin beams on the medal stand after winning gold in the 100-meter backstroke event at the 2004 Olympics in Athens, Greece.*

freestyle relay and in the 4 x 100 individual medley relay, and a bronze medal in the 100-meter freestyle. This made her the third American woman in history to win five medals at a single Olympics. Moreover, when she won the gold medal for the 100-meter backstroke, she was the first American female Olympian at the 2004 games to win a gold medal. She considers winning that medal one of the most memorable experiences of her life. "I've been through a lot, and it means so much more to have won an . . . Olympic gold medal," Coughlin told reporters. "No matter what happens in my career now, I'll always have an Olympic gold medal."[45]

Leaving Athens, Coughlin had no idea where her career as a professional athlete would take her. There would be more gold medals, more accolades, and opportunities to do things she never even dreamed about. She still had a long way to go.

# International Celebrity

After the 2004 Olympics, Coughlin was treated with a measure of celebrity few swimmers receive. People recognized her on the street and asked for her autograph, and flight attendants announced her presence on whatever flight she boarded. Her Olympic success, good looks, poise, and grace made her a favorite with the media and the public. She made the rounds of television talk shows and was the subject of print and Internet articles and magazine photo spreads. At the same time, her responsibility to her sponsors kept her busy making guest appearances and commercials. It was an exhausting schedule, but it presented Coughlin with many new and interesting opportunities. Some celebrities might have complained, but Coughlin enjoyed all the activity. As she explains, "there was that sense of urgency that I needed to do as many appearances as possible right after the Olympics. But so many of them were really fun. I didn't see it as pressure, but my schedule was incredibly hectic."[46]

## A Three-Month Break

Despite her hectic schedule, Coughlin continued to train with McKeever in preparation for an autumn meet. Once the meet was over, Coughlin planned to take a break from the pool and restrict her training to dry land. That break happened sooner than she expected. One morning in October 2004, as she ran

*Coughlin walks the red carpet at an ESPN event in New York City in September 2004, one of several public appearances she made to capitalize on her Olympic success.*

across the pool deck, she felt a sharp pain in her left foot. She had a stress fracture. A stress fracture is a small crack in a bone that is usually caused by overuse of the bone. Stress fractures of the foot are common among runners. Coughlin cross trained by running six days a week.

Wearing a walking boot and using a cane for support, she continued to make appearances for her sponsors. But the injury forced Coughlin to stop training entirely for the next three months. In some respects, it was a blessing in disguise. It forced her to reduce her frenetic schedule, giving her a chance to relax and unwind while she healed. "In a way it was perfect timing," she later told a reporter. "During my time off I'd planned to run and do Pilates, but with the broken foot that wasn't an option. The only workouts I could've done would have been in the pool. So I decided to be lazy until January."[47] While she was healing, she and Hall adopted a border terrier puppy, which they named She-Ra. The couple had lots of fun training and playing with the pup. Coughlin also spent time socializing with her friends and family. One of the high points of the period was attending the big college graduation party that Coughlin's family threw for her.

## Relaxing Hobbies

Coughlin also pursued her two hobbies—cooking and photography. Coughlin got her first camera when she was a little girl and had been snapping pictures ever since. She took a photography class in college in which she learned to develop black-and-white film. She was also adept at digital photography. Her work was so good that a close friend who was getting married asked her to be her official wedding photographer. Coughlin did an excellent job but prefers photographing nature to people. She posts many of her photos on Facebook, Twitter, and her website.

Coughlin also often posts original recipes online. She developed a passion for cooking in college. But her interest in cooking began when she was a little girl. She loved to watch her mother and grandmother cook. She enjoyed watching cooking programs

*An avid cook, Coughlin demonstrates her skills in a segment on* **Today** *with hosts Savannah Guthrie, left, Natalie Morales, and Al Roker in August 2012.*

on television, too. In fact, as children, she and her sister often watched the Food Network together.

Cooking relaxed Coughlin and let her be creative. She tried many different recipes and became knowledgeable about nutrition and healthy eating. Soon, she was experimenting with her own recipes and serving the best results at dinner parties she gave for her friends. Coughlin and Hall like to entertain.

Coughlin enjoys eating. She does not like counting calories or overanalyzing her diet the way many athletes do. She believes that these practices make eating less pleasurable. Cooking has made Coughlin more knowledgeable about food and how to best fuel her body for peak performance so she does not have to count calories or analyze her diet. As she explains,

> When it comes to food they [athletes] can think a lot about calories and protein grams and break foods into

micronutrients. It's important to know the basics of what minerals and nutrients are in food. I think it takes the pleasure out of food when you break it down too much—it's almost like a science project. For the most part, I think it's good to eat a wide variety of fruits and vegetables and whole grains. I think food is something pleasurable. I enjoy eating and it makes me happy. I also try to eat healthfully, but at the same time I don't think of counting every single calorie or gram of protein. I don't worry about things nearly as much as some athletes. You have to educate yourself about foods and how they're made, and I think cooking is a great way to do that because you see what goes into every one of those dishes.[48]

Realizing how much she enjoyed her hobbies, she made a point of finding time for them once she resumed training. Now that she was no longer a student, she needed activities other than swimming to stimulate her and enrich her life. It also helped her to take her mind off swimming and the stress of being a professional athlete. As she explains, "I think it is really important to have hobbies outside my sport. If I was just thinking about swimming 24–7 [24 hours a day, 7 days a week], I'd go insane. I'm very much a type A personality [a perfectionist] and I can get very, very obsessive. So it keeps me sane and keeps me focused on something other than my sport."[49]

## Opening Up

Coughlin was also involved in other activities, including coauthoring a book about her life with writer Michael Silver. The book began as a standard biography about a popular athlete. It became much more as Coughlin opened up about her life, her negative experiences in youth swimming, and her strong feelings concerning the rigid way most young swimmers are trained. According to Silver,

the story I wrote isn't the story I set out to write. What I had in mind was not nearly as compelling as what I wrote.

Coughlin's biography, published in 2006, recounts the stress and stringency of her teenage years as a member of the Terrapins, the details of which caused a stir in the swimming world.

I ended up with a better story about a sport, swimming, because of Natalie. . . . [My] original lure was Natalie who I had met and I was drawn to her likeability and cool personality. We met for lunch several times and it was Natalie who opened up to tell her full story. I'm proud of Natalie for telling her story. She hopes it will be beneficial to the next generation of swimmers.[50]

It was not easy for Coughlin to relive painful moments from her past. At first, she shied away from talking about her final years with the Terrapins. But the more she thought about it the more she realized it was an integral part of her story. Plus, her treatment was typical of the stringent youth swimming culture that she wanted to expose and see changed. As she explains,

at first, I was like, why does it have to be in there? I knew how some people were going to react. Then it made sense. I had to say why I was burned out. . . . I remember how I felt at 16 and 17. There were so many days I came home crying. I wanted to quit so badly. There are so many other swimmers that felt that way. . . . If I hadn't talked about that, my story wouldn't make sense. I need to say that I haven't swum for [Coach Ray Mitchell] in six years. I made some of my closest friends with the Terrapins, and I cherished it. But I just disagreed with his methods and how we were treated. For every success story, there are a lot of girls who leave completely bitter. That's so sad.[51]

The book caused a stir in the swimming community. Some of Coughlin's former teammates posted a response to the book on the Terrapin's website in which they disputed her less-than-flattering portrayal of Mitchell and the team. The team also hired a lawyer to look into the possibility of suing Coughlin, but the team never pursued it. Coughlin was aware that her revelations would likely infuriate many people. She did not want to hurt anyone. Still, she did what she thought was right. It took courage for her to do so. She does not regret her actions, just as she does not regret many of her other unpopular choices. In talking about Coughlin,

Silver says that her most defining characteristic is her courage to do what she believes in. As he explains,

> she has this sort of intuitive conviction about her, an unwavering sense of what is right for her and the courage to stick to her guns even when her choices are unpopular—fighting with her parents for the right to attend [Berkeley] instead of Stanford; forging, along with Teri McKeever, an alternative training approach; turning down big endorsement dollars to stay in school for her senior year; choosing Janey Miller as her agent instead of the big guns like Octagon; insisting on swimming the more competitive 100-meter freestyle instead of the 200-meter backstroke, which was considered a sure gold; sublimating her individual aspirations in order to swim on all three relays; and, most of all, being willing to put out a book that will rile many members of the swimming establishment.[52]

## Broadcaster

Coughlin's next opportunity did not require the same type of courage. It came her way when MSNBC offered her a chance to contribute to the on-air coverage of the 2006 Winter Olympics. Although she did not travel to Torino, Italy, where the games were held, she was an in-studio guest analyst. In her role, she gave on-air commentary of the events from an Olympian's point of view and interviewed athletes via satellite. Coughlin enjoyed the experience so much that she has considered pursuing a career in broadcasting or acting when she retires from swimming. As she told Olympic historian and blogger Nicholas Wolaver, "[I] would love to do something in TV if the opportunity came along."[53]

## Role Model

Being in the spotlight affected Coughlin's life in other ways. Many young people look up to professional athletes and want to be just like them, especially when the athletes receive lots of media

# Sports-Related Careers

**M**any people dream of becoming a professional athlete, but few actually achieve their dreams. There are many sports-related careers that allow sports fans to work in the field they love. Among these are careers in sports training, such as athletic trainers, personal trainers, strength and conditioning coaches, and fitness instructors. These individuals are involved in the development of an athlete's strength, speed, and stamina. They access an athlete's body then plan and implement a training program for the athlete based on their individual needs. Physical education teachers, too, train athletes. They teach young people about fitness, health, and sports.

Exercise physiology is another sports-related career. Exercise physiologists are experts in the science of exercise. An exercise physiologist may design training programs and fitness tests, conduct scientific research, or work with injured athletes. Physical therapists also work with injured athletes. Doctors who specialize in sports medicine also deal with an athlete's physical health. Sports psychologists deal with an athlete's mental well-being.

Sportswriting is another choice. Sportswriters write about sports, while sports analysts, announcers, and commentators report on sports on radio and television. Sports photographers get into the action by taking pictures of sporting events.

attention. Coughlin took being a role model for young people seriously. She tried to set a good example in the way she lived her life, and in the way she contributed to helping improve the lives of children. Coughlin volunteered to be an athlete ambassador for Right To Play, a charitable organization that uses sports and play to help children in some of the most disadvantaged communities in the world to learn life skills involving health, decision making, cooperation, leadership, tolerance, conflict resolution, and teamwork. The organization contends that these lessons have a positive and lasting impact on the children's future and the future of their communities.

As an athlete ambassador, Coughlin helped promote the charity. According to the Right To Play website,

Athlete Ambassadors are volunteers and role models who inspire and celebrate children. They lend their time to raise awareness about our cause. They attend Right To Play events and promote fundraising campaigns in traditional and social media. When an Athlete Ambassador is able to visit programs to witness Right To Play's work with children, they play an important role in spreading the word about the impact of play on education, health and life skills.[54]

Coughlin took her role in supporting the charity so seriously that she donated twenty thousand dollars of her 2008 Olympic gold medal winnings to the organization. She and Chinese diver Gao Min served as representatives of the charity at the 2008 Olympic Games.

## Experience Counts

While still pursuing her other activities, Coughlin resumed training once her foot healed. Her focus was the 2008 Olympics in Beijing. This time, she hoped to swim in three individual events—the 100-meter backstroke, the 100-meter freestyle, and the 200-meter individual medley, as well as in three relays. But first she had to win a place at the Olympic trials in Omaha, Nebraska, a task that Coughlin made look simple. Her performance at the trials was spectacular. Not only did she qualify for the Olympics in all her events, but she also broke the world record for the 100-meter backstroke for the third time in her swimming career, completing the race in an astounding 58.96 seconds. She told the press after the trials,

I feel great. I've never had so many lifetime bests in my adult career. I'm swimming personal bests in the [100-meter backstroke], the [100-meter] freestyle and the [200-meter individual medley] and those are my three individual events in Beijing. Hopefully, I will be on three relays as well. So I have a full schedule in Beijing, but I'm excited about the challenge and I think I'll fare pretty well.[55]

*Coughlin swims at a world-record pace in the 100-meter backstroke finals at the Olympic trials in June 2008.*

## Team Leader

Coughlin went to Beijing feeling less pressure than she had going to Athens. She had already shown her spirit to the world. This time she had nothing to prove. As she explained in an interview,

> I feel like I have less pressure this time, just because the way swimming works is you're validated through the Olympics and you only have that opportunity every four years. Going into the last Olympics I remember having these interviews where the interviewer would say, oh you have world records and American records but you don't have that gold, and things like that and it puts so much pressure on me to get that Olympic medal and I feel like I've done that. And now I can just focus on myself in the next games.[56]

Coughlin's role in Beijing, however, was not without any pressure. She was named cocaptain of the women's Olympic swim team along with Dara Torres and Amanda Beard. Torres and Beard had participated in a combined nine Olympics, while Coughlin was just returning to her second Olympics. This was a tremendous honor for Coughlin and a testament to how much the swimming community valued her leadership skills. As team co-captain, she served as a role model and mentor to the younger, less-experienced team members.

## Olympic Firsts

Before leaving for Beijing, Coughlin received another honor. She was asked to carry the Olympic torch in San Francisco as part of the torch's ritual journey around the world. Once at the games, Coughlin's focus turned to swimming. Earning medals in all six of her events would not be easy. The 100-meter backstroke, Coughlin's best and favorite event, would prove to be particularly challenging.

Coughlin entered the semifinals of the event as the world record holder. However, Zimbabwe's Kristy Coventry, who got the silver medal in the 100-meter backstroke in Athens, managed to break Coughlin's record and finish first. She had to beat Coventry to get the gold medal. Using her powerful kick to propel her, Coughlin swam her hardest. Her legs hurt so badly from the effort that she bit her lips until they bled to distract her mind from the pain. When she touched the wall, she doubted she had won. Her time was 58.96 seconds.

To her surprise, Coughlin had won. She explains, "When I saw the clock I thought I had made a mistake and I only knew I had won when I saw the number one by my name. It's a great feeling, I am overjoyed."[57]

Her win made Coughlin the first woman in Olympic history to win successive titles in the event. At the medals ceremony, she was overcome by emotions. She could not control the tears of joy that streamed down her face. "To win gold in such a strong event, I'm so proud. That's probably why I was crying like a baby up on the stand,"[58] she told reporters.

Before the games ended, Coughlin had a lot more to be proud of. She won medals in all six of her events, winning silver in the

*A tearful Coughlin shows off her gold medal after winning the 100-meter backstroke event at the Olympics in 2008. She was the first woman in Olympic history to win successive titles in the event.*

# The Physics of Swimming

**W**ater is seven hundred times denser than air. Swimmers must deal with drag or resistance as they move through the water. There are three types of drag that act on a swimmer: frictional, wave, and form. Frictional drag is the result of the interaction between an object's surface texture (a swimmer's clothes, skin, and body hair) and the water. Frictional drag slows swimmers down. Wearing smooth, form-fitting swimwear, a swim cap, and shaving body hair help minimize frictional drag.

Wave drag occurs when swimmers move through water, creating waves. The more the swimmer splashes the greater the waves and the resistance or drag. Swimmers with smoother strokes create less wave drag. Lane ropes between swim lanes also help reduce wave drag.

Form drag is resistance caused by the swimmer's body shape as it moves through the water. Form drag varies depending on a person's body shape. Larger people create more drag. Keeping the body straight and tight with arms overhead and toes pointed helps reduce form drag.

4 x 100 freestyle relay and the 4 x 100 medley relay and bronze in the 200-meter individual medley, the 100-meter freestyle, and the 4 x 200 freestyle relay. Her performance made her the first American woman in an Olympic sport to win six medals in one Olympics.

The four years between the 2004 and 2008 Olympics were some of the best in Coughlin's life so far. She took advantage of the many opportunities her celebrity status brought her and she cultivated the hobbies she enjoyed. When the 2008 Olympics drew near, she trained harder than ever. The result was an Olympic performance that went down in history and made Coughlin a superstar.

# Chapter 5

# A Balanced Life

After the Olympics, the United States Olympic Committee named Coughlin its 2008 Sports Woman of the Year. This was a great honor for Coughlin personally and for the sport of swimming. Coughlin had done a lot to raise public interest in swimming. The sport had also done a lot for her. But training for the Olympics and swimming in multiple races had taken a lot out of her. She decided to take an eighteen-month break from swimming to reflect on her past accomplishments, to savor the present, and to think about the future. She remained in shape by running an average of 9 miles (14km) a day, dancing, lifting weights, and doing Pilates. Coughlin found that maintaining a balance between her career as a professional athlete and her personal life kept her healthy and happy.

## Getting Married

Before the Olympics, Coughlin and Hall bought a small house in the hills of Lafayette, California, not far from Berkeley. In April 2008 Hall proposed to Coughlin in the garden of their new home. The couple had been together since they were teenagers. They were good friends, sharing many mutual interests. As a swimmer, Hall understood the challenges Coughlin faced and provided her with all the love and support she needed. Of course, Coughlin said "yes," to Hall's proposal. Planning their wedding was first on Coughlin's post-Olympic agenda.

The couple decided on an outdoor wedding. It was held on the scenic grounds of the Carneros Inn in Napa, California, on

April 25, 2009. As the guests arrived, they were served fresh-squeezed lemonade and guided to an apple orchard, where the elegant but quirky ceremony took place. The bridal party, which included traditional bridesmaids and groomsmen, also included the couple's border terrier, She-Ra, dressed in a miniature bridal gown and bridal veil. Not to be outdone, Coughlin wore a sleeveless, open-backed, lace gown by fashion designer Monique Lhuillier. She wore gardenias in her hair and carried a bouquet of white roses and peonies wrapped in green silk. She looked beautiful as she exchanged her vows with Hall.

After the ceremony, a party was held in the courtyard of the inn. Twinkling lights were strung in the trees, and a big fire burned in an outdoor fireplace. The guests were treated to steaks or sea bass, followed by wedding cupcakes. The couple spent the night at the inn and then honeymooned in Hawaii where they relaxed, surfed, and swam with dolphins.

## Urban Farmer

When Coughlin and Hall bought their house in Lafayette, one of the deciding factors in selecting that particular house was its large yard. There Coughlin could plant a garden. She had grown herbs in flowerpots on the terrace of her condo. The next step was a full-scale garden in which she could grow fresh ingredients to use in her cooking. She explains,

> When I was a kid, I had a 90-year-old neighbor—she could stick anything in the ground and it would grow and flourish. We'd always play in her garden. I still have the colander that she used to make potpourri from her roses. A lot of people in my life have had backyard gardens, so when I was looking to buy a home, that was one of the requirements.[59]

Coughlin's garden started out small but has grown considerably over the years. She tends her own little orchard where she grows figs, lemons, peaches, and oranges. She also has seven vegetable beds in which she rotates a variety of herbs, berries, and vegetables. She explains,

*Coughlin poses in the garden she tends in the backyard of her home in Lafayette, California.*

Gardening has been something that has evolved out of my love of food. Often times a homegrown veggie or fruit is far tastier than anything you can buy at a store because it's picked at its peak of ripeness. I grow most of my veggies from seed and never use any pesticides or herbicides. I have two rules when deciding what to put in my garden: Grow what you love and grow what you can't buy otherwise.[60]

Coughlin also added five chickens to what she calls her urban farm. The chickens are both pets and suppliers of fresh eggs. "Chickens," she explains, "are probably the easiest pet you can have. You just provide them with shelter, food, water, and protection and they're happy. We get three to eight beautiful eggs a day—greenish-blue eggs, pinkish-brown eggs—and they're as fresh as they could possibly be. They're better than anything you can get in the stores."[61]

Coughlin fully enjoys the bounty of her garden by not letting any of her crops go to waste. Whatever she and Hall do not eat fresh, she preserves by freezing, pickling, and canning.

## The Edible Schoolyard

One of Coughlin's inspirations for gardening and healthy eating is Alice Waters, a famous Berkeley chef who uses only fresh, locally grown ingredients in her restaurant. In 1996 Waters started the Edible Schoolyard at Berkeley's Martin Luther King Jr. Middle School. It is a 1-acre (0.4ha) garden with a kitchen classroom, where children are actively involved in growing and cooking their own school lunches. Coughlin is a big supporter of the Edible Schoolyard. With other volunteers, she helps weed and maintain the garden.

Coughlin also supports healthy eating and cooking in other ways. In 2009 she became a spokesperson for the California Dried Plum Board. Dried plums are Coughlin's favorite snack. She has eaten the fruit, which is considered a superfood because it is loaded with disease fighting nutrients, all her life. As she explains, "it [dried plums] was something that I'd always eaten throughout my career. I just snack with them mostly. I do enjoy cooking with them quite a bit. I like adding sweetness to savory dishes. I like balancing the flavors that way, but I just keep them with me in my gym bags. I keep them in the glove compartment of my car."[62]

Coughlin's passion for healthy eating and healthy living also got her involved in First Lady Michelle Obama's Let's Move campaign. It is a program designed to combat childhood obesity by promoting healthy eating and living. In 2012 Mrs. Obama attended an event designed to publicize the collaboration between the United States Olympic Committee and the Let's Move program. There were about two dozen Olympians at the event. Coughlin was chosen from all of

*Coughlin hugs Michelle Obama at a U.S. Olympic Committee event at which the first lady promoted her Let's Move campaign in May 2012.*

them to introduce Mrs. Obama. The usually laid-back Coughlin was so nervous about meeting Mrs. Obama that she was visibly shaking. The First Lady gave Coughlin a big hug to help calm her down. It was a great honor for Coughlin, one she will never forget.

## Dancing with the Stars

Coughlin had another unforgettable experience in the fall of 2009, when she was invited to be a contestant on *Dancing with the Stars*, a reality television show in which celebrities, paired with professional dancers, perform predetermined dances. Each couple competes against the other couples for judges' points and audience votes. Each week, the couple that receives the lowest combined total of points and votes is eliminated until three couples remain who are judged third, second, and first place winners of the competition. Coughlin, who studied dance as a child and loves to dance, jumped at the opportunity. "I wanted to dance my entire life," she told a reporter. "If I wasn't a swimmer, I would have been a dancer."[63]

Coughlin was paired with professional dancer Alec Mazo. The two got along very well. Coughlin enjoyed the challenge of learning the dances and the competitive nature of the program. The hours of physically intense training delighted her. She explains, "The training was awesome. That was my favorite part—just working so hard with Alec for a purpose."[64]

Out of sixteen couples, Coughlin and Mazo were eliminated sixth. *Dancing with the Stars* judge Carrie Ann Inaba was sorry to see her go. "I was a little disappointed," Inaba explains. "We haven't had a female dancer who moved with so much strength and flexibility and fluidity in a while. And she hasn't had any performing experience, I was really excited to see how far she could grow throughout the ten weeks of the show."[65]

**Coughlin performs on Dancing with the Stars with professional partner Alec Mazo, left, in September 2009.**

Coughlin was also disappointed. As she told talk show host Jay Leno, "I was kind of depressed for a couple of days because you get sucked into this reality [television] world and you think that it's life or death, and then you snap out of it. My husband was like, what . . . is wrong with you? For about three days, I was pretty depressed then I was like wait—it was a fun dance competition."[66]

Despite her disappointment, Coughlin says that the experience was great. She learned many new dance steps, which she experiments with whenever she dances with her husband. She especially likes spinning and turning. She insists that she would love to compete on *Dancing with the Stars* again if the opportunity arises. Next time, this fierce competitor just might win.

## Body Painting

In participating in *Dancing with the Stars*, Coughlin stepped out of her comfort zone and did something new and daring. It turned out to be so much fun that in 2012 she once again decided to try something different. She agreed to be a model in *Sports Illustrated Swimsuit Edition*. What made her decision especially bold was that she and two other female athletes were featured wearing body paint rather than actual swimsuits. Using layer upon layer of special paint, artist Joanne Gair, painted a reproduction of a Speedo swimsuit on Coughlin's nude body. The process took about ten hours, during which time Coughlin had to stand still. The end result was amazing. It is almost impossible to tell that Coughlin is not wearing a real swimsuit. Says Coughlin, "It's one thing to see it on print but to see it in person, it's such a work of art and I felt horrible washing it off afterwards."[67]

Coughlin was fascinated by the body painting experience. Moreover, since she looked clothed in the photographs, she did not feel that she was doing anything contrary to her principles. In fact, she felt she was sending a message to young women that all types of bodies are beautiful, not just model-thin ones. As she explains, "as beautiful as the supermodels are, I think it's great to have different types of bodies. To have an athletic body

# American Women and the 2012 Olympics

A merican female athletes dominated the 2012 Olympics. They won a total of fifty-eight medals, thirteen more than American men. The women's total medal count was even better than the total medal count for most countries. Only China with eighty-eight medals, Russia with eighty-two medals, and Great Britain with sixty-five medals had more.

Twenty-nine of the American women's medals are gold medals. Only China and Great Britain won as many gold medals. Among the American women's most memorable performances was that of the gymnastic team, which won the team competition. The women's soccer, basketball, and water polo teams also took home gold medals.

Individual female athletes also shined brightly. Sixteen-year-old gymnast Gabby Douglas stunned the world when she won the individual all-around competition. Seventeen-year-old swimmer Missy Franklin won five medals and broke two world records. Women also did well in track and field, with stars like Allyson Felix winning three gold medals and Sanya Richards-Ross taking home two.

Since many of these athletes are so young, they are likely to compete at the Summer Olympics in 2016 and make America proud once again.

in [Sports Illustrated] Swimsuit Issue, I think, is really important. [Sports Illustrated] is a sports magazine in the first place. So it's nice to have balance between models and athletes."[68]

## Back in the Pool

In the midst of all her other activities, Coughlin got back in the pool in January 2010 with an eye on the 2012 Olympics in London. After being out of the water for over a year, she did not

*Captured with an underwater camera, Coughlin competes in a heat of the 100-meter freestyle event at the World Championships in July 2011, at which she won three medals.*

know whether she would be able to swim with her former speed and technique. But her dry land training had paid off, and she was pleased to see that she still had the makings of a champion. At the same time, she was well aware that she had a lot to work on. As she explained at the time, "I feel like I'm very physically fit and ready to go. But there are little things that just aren't quite there yet. Judging the flags, judging your distance from the wall into turns—things like that have been a little off for me."[69] Even so, she won three medals at the 2011 World Championships, a gold in the medley relay, a silver in the 400-meter freestyle relay, and a bronze in the 100-meter backstroke.

As the Olympic trials drew closer, Coughlin revved up her training. Coughlin described an average day to Leno in this way:

> I generally wake up at 4:30, have breakfast #1, get to the pool by 5 A.M., do Pilates, listen to a podcast, then I swim for two hours. Then I lift [weights] for an hour and a half; then I have breakfast #2 and then I go back and swim again; then I do another Pilates class. [I train for] about five or six hours a day, and I like to go to bed very early and have dinner at 4 o'clock.[70]

# "Icing on the Cake"

Coughlin's goal was to make the 2012 Olympic team. In order to do that, she had to get through the Olympic trials successfully. She would be competing against a strong field of contenders, including a crop of remarkable teenagers. Now twenty-nine years old, Coughlin was one of the older contenders. Still, having already achieved so much, Coughlin knew that whatever happened, she would be proud of herself. "This is all icing on the cake," she said at the time. "I really want to be there [at the Olympics] representing my country, but if I don't, I don't, and life will go on."[71]

Coughlin did not fare as well as she hoped at the trials. Although she had the second fastest time of the year in the 100-meter butterfly going into the trials, she came in fourth in the

*Coughlin crouches to dive into the pool at the start of her leg of the 4 x 100 freestyle relay semifinals at the 2012 Olympics in London, England. Her team earned a silver medal in the event.*

finals. More shocking, she came in third in the 100-meter backstroke, the event in which Coughlin had previously won back-to-back Olympic gold medals. She finished behind teenagers Missy Franklin and Rachel Bootsma, both of whom considered Coughlin to be their role model. The press watched Coughlin closely to see how she would react to the loss. She immediately swam over to the two young winners and embraced them, telling them how proud she was of their performance. The media, she explains, "expected me to throw some big hissy fit. It's just a race. I was truly happy for Boots and Missy."[72]

Coughlin's last chance to make the team was the 100-meter freestyle. She started the race strong but finished weak, coming

# Tapering

Natalie Coughlin thinks that her poor performance at the 2012 Olympics trials was due to overtraining, or insufficient tapering. *Tapering* is a term used by swimmers that describes the period before a major swim meet when swimmers reduce their level of training. Tapering allows swimmer's bodies to rest, to increase energy level, and amp up performance. When swimmers taper, they do not stop training entirely. They just rest more and train less vigorously.

To get the best results, the timing of tapering is vital. If the period of time in which a swimmer tapers is too long, the swimmer may be out of shape by the time of the meet. If it is too short, the swimmer may be overtired. Coughlin attributes her lack of success at the trials to the latter. Depending on the individual, tapering can last anywhere from a few days to six weeks. It is up to the coach and the swimmer to decide how much tapering the swimmer needs.

in sixth. It was not good enough to qualify for the individual event, but it did put her on the six-member 4 x 100 freestyle relay team. She was officially a third time Olympian and a second-time captain of the team.

Coughlin was disappointed with her performance at the trials. She attributed her poor showing to overtraining, which can weaken an athlete's performance. But she was happy to be on the team and relished her role mentoring the younger athletes. "This isn't the meet I visualized or anticipated going into this year," she told reporters right after making the team. "[But making the team is] awesome, a huge honor. . . . I'll be there to support my teammates and the rest of Team U.S.A., and I think that will be my bigger role at this Olympics."[73]

The 4 x 100 freestyle relay was held on the first day of the Olympics. Coughlin swam in the preliminary race, clocking the fastest American time in her leg of the relay. But McKeever, the women's team head coach, chose four younger swimmers for the finals. Coughlin stayed in the stands and cheered as the team swam to a bronze medal finish. In a relay, the participants in the preliminary race and the finals all earn a medal. Coughlin had earned her twelfth Olympic medal, tying with Dara Torres and Jenny Thompson as the most decorated American female Olympian in history.

## What the Future Holds

Upon returning from London, Coughlin's responsibilities to her sponsors and her popularity with the media kept her busy. In her spare time, she worked in her garden, tried new recipes, and socialized with family and friends. She and Hall went on a great white shark cage-diving adventure in Mexico, something Coughlin wanted to do all her life. It was an incredible experience, which she documented with dozens of underwater photographs. She also went on a trip to Rwanda to do field work for Right To Play.

Many people believed she would retire from swimming after the London Olympics. But Coughlin is unsure if she is ready to do so. "I'm having fun," she explains, "and I'm lucky to be a professional athlete, which is the best job in the world."[74] In fact, Coughlin is considering training for the 2016 Olympics in Brazil. If she does not make the team, Coughlin is unsure what she will do. But she does have some ideas. She likes the ideas of hosting a television cooking show and of writing a cookbook. She is also open to a career in sportscasting or acting. And, she and Hall have long considered starting their own youth swimming school. Someday, the couple hopes to start a family. But no matter what the future holds for Coughlin, swimming will always be an important part of her life.

# Introduction: Pretty Tough

1. Quoted in Kelli Anderson. "The Next Golden Girl." *Sports Illustrated*, July 28, 2003. http://sportsillustrated.cnn.com/vault/article/magazine/MAG1029211/index/index.htm.
2. Quoted in John Crumpacker. "World Record Holder Natalie Coughlin Provides 'Food for Thought.'" California Golden Bears, January 27, 2003. http://www.calbears.com/sports/w-swim/spec-rel/012703aab.html.
3. Michael Silver. "My Sportsman Choice: Natalie Coughlin." *Sports Illustrated*, November 17, 2004. http://sportsillustrated.cnn.com/2004/magazine/specials/sportsman/2004/11/17/silver.coughlin.
4. Quoted in Mike Dodd. "Swimmer Coughlin Poised for Pedestal." *USA Today*, August 1, 2004. www.usatoday.com/sports/olympics/athens/swimming/2004-08-01-coughlin-cover_x.htm#.
5. Quoted in Anderson. "The Next Golden Girl."
6. Quoted in Jane. "The Sweet Life of Natalie Coughlin." Pretty Tough, January 15, 2011. www.prettytough.com/the-sweet-life-of-natalie-coughlin.
7. Quoted in Anderson. "The Next Golden Girl."
8. Cynthia Gorney. "A Feel for the Water." *New Yorker*, July 5, 2004. http://www.newyorker.com/archive/2004/07/05/040705fa_fact_gorney.

# Chapter 1: "I'm a Water Baby"

9. Quoted in Gorney. "A Feel for the Water."
10. Quoted in Jill Lieber. "Coughlin Healed up, Geared Up." *USA Today*, August 11, 2002. http://www.usatoday.com/sports/olympics/summer/2002-08-11-coughlin-cover_x.htm.
11. Quoted in Mel Orpilla. "Natalie Coughlin: Olympic Hero." Orpilla.com. www.orpilla.com/natalie.html.

12. Quoted in "Natalie Coughlin 2012 Olympic Preview: GMM Presented by SwimOutlet.com." You Tube. http://www.youtube.com/watch?v=rj_w4XKFLDs.
13. Quoted in Dodd. "Swimmer Coughlin Poised for Pedestal."
14. Quoted in Anderson. "The Next Golden Girl."
15. Quoted in Orpilla. "Natalie Coughlin."
16. Quoted in Michael Silver. *Golden Girl.* With Natalie Coughlin. Emmaus, PA: Rodale, 2006. p. 38.
17. Quoted in Orpilla. "Natalie Coughlin."
18. Quoted in Frank Litsky. "Swimming: U.S. Spring National Championship; Talented Teen-Ager to Compete Today." *New York Times*, March 29, 1999. http://www.nytimes.com/1999/03/29/sports/swimming-us-spring-national-championships-talented-teen-ager-to-compete-today.html.
19. Quoted in Gorney. "A Feel for the Water."
20. Quoted in Gorney. "A Feel for the Water."
21. Quoted in Anderson. "The Next Golden Girl."
22. Quoted in Josh Jeffrey. "Female High School Swimmer of the Year: Natalie Coughlin." *Swimming World*, August 1, 1998. http://www.swimmingworldmagazine.com/articles/swimmingworld/articles/199808-01sw_art.asp.
23. Quoted in Silver. *Golden Girl*, p. 41.
24. Quoted in Silver. *Golden Girl*, p. 44.
25. Quoted in Dodd. "Swimmer Coughlin Poised for Pedestal."
26. Silver. *Golden Girl*, p. 47.
27. Silver. *Golden Girl*, p. 44–45.
28. Quoted in Anderson. "The Next Golden Girl."

## Chapter 2: Making Waves

29. Quoted in Nico Ferrara. "US Olympic Swim Team Coach: HTE Interview!" Here There Everywhere, April 10, 2012. http://htekidsnews.com/us-olympic-swim-team-coach-hte-interview.
30. Quoted in Lieber. "Coughlin Healed up, Geared Up."
31. Quoted in Gorney. "A Feel for the Water."

32. Quoted in Bob Schaller. "20 Question Tuesday: Natalie Coughlin." USA Swimming, April 12, 2011. http://www.usaswimming.org/ViewNewsArticle.aspx?TabId=0&itemid=3283&mid=8712.

33. Quoted in Daniel Duane. "Water Baby." *Men's Vogue*, April 2008, 102.

34. Quoted in Ferrara. "US Olympic Swim Team Coach."

35. Quoted in Bob Schaller. "Setting the Bar High: Natalie Coughlin." *Splash*. http://www.bobschaller.com/SplashNat.pdf.

36. Quoted in Peter Crooks. "Gold Medal Gourmet." *Diablo*, November 2008. http://www.diablomag.com/Diablo-Magazine/November-2008/Gold-Medal-Gourmet.

37. Quoted in Jeffrey Kahn. "Berkeley's Natalie Coughlin: Destined to Swim." University of California, Berkeley, April 4, 2002. http://berkeley.edu/news/media/releases/2002/04/08_coughlin.html.

38. Quoted in Kahn. "Berkeley's Natalie Coughlin."

# Chapter 3: America's Golden Girl

39. Silver. *Golden Girl*, pp. 12–13.

40. Quoted in Silver. *Golden Girl*, p. 144.

41. Quoted in Silver. "My Sportsman Choice."

42. Quoted in Tyler Kepner. "Summer 2004 Games: Swimming: Women's 100-Meter Backstroke; After Limiting Her Schedule, Coughlin Turns in Winning Start," NYTimes.com, August 17, 2004. http://www.nytimes.com/2004/08/17/sports/summer-2004-games-swimming-women-s-100-meter-backstroke-after-limiting-her.html?ref=nataliecoughlin#.

43. Silver, *Golden Girl*, p. 227.

44. Quoted in John Crumpacker. "Natalie Coughlin Already a Star, Readying for International Stage." *San Francisco Chronicle*, July 6, 2004.

45. Quoted in Crumpacker. "Natalie Coughlin Already a Star, Readying for International Stage."

# Chapter 4: International Celebrity

46. Quoted in Richard Deitsch. "Q & A: Natalie Coughlin." *Sports Illustrated*, May 8, 2006. http://sportsillustrated.cnn.com/vault/article/magazine/MAG1111109/index.htm.

47. Quoted in Michael Silver. "Return of the Water Warrior." *Sports Illustrated*, July 25, 2005. http://sportsillustrated.cnn.com/vault/article/magazine/MAG1108774/index.htm.

48. Quoted in Jeannine Stein. "Olympian Natalie Coughlin on Food: Eat Healthfully, but Enjoy It." *Los Angeles Times*, January 31, 2012. http://articles.latimes.com/2012/jan/31/news/la-heb-natalie-coughlin-food-nutrition-20120131.

49. "Natalie Coughlin: Wedding Photographer." YouTube Video, 1:01. Posted by "2012NBCOlympics," May 7, 2012. http://www.youtube.com/watch?v=3cnyokBC3SE.

50. Quoted in Ivette Ricco. "Exclusive Interview with Natalie Coughlin: The Golden Girl." August 9, 2006. FemmeFan.com, www.femmefan.com/site/featuredarticles/06_07Season/interview%20with%20Natalie%20Coughlin.htm.

51. Quoted in Jennifer Starks. "Next Chapter: Swimmer, Olympic Gold Medalist Savors Success, Tells All in New Book," *Contra Costa Times* (Walnut Creek, CA), June 2, 2006.

52. Quoted in B. Redman. "Michael Silver Talks About Golden Girl." Book Help Web. http://book.consumerhelpweb.com/authors/silver/interview.htm.

53. Quoted in Nicholas Wolaver. "Olympian Interview: Natalie Coughlin." Olympic Rings and Other Things, March 26, 2011. http://olympicringsandotherthings.blogspot.com/2011/03/olympian-interview-natalie-coughlin.html.

54. "Our Athletes." Right To Play. http://www.righttoplay.com/International/the-team/Pages/OurAthletes.aspx.

55. Quoted in "Natalie Coughlin: Aiming to Raise the Bar." ABC.net, July 23, 2008. http://www.abc.net.au/news/stories/2008/07/23/2311814.htm?site=olympics/2008/athletes.

56. Quoted in "Natalie Coughlin Interview." *Beatweek Magazine*, August 22, 2008. http://www.beatweek.com/iphone/ipodiphoneitunes/66-interview-with-natalie-coughlin.

57. Quoted in Agence France-Presse. "Coughlin Trumps Coventry." *South China Morning Post*, August 12, 2008. http://olympics. scmp.com/Article.aspx?id=2425&section=latestnews.

58. Quoted in Agence France-Presse. "Coughlin Trumps Coventry."

# Chapter 5: A Balanced Life

59. Quoted in Avital Binshtock Andrews. "Trendsetter: Natalie Coughlin." Sierra Club. www.sierraclub.org/sierra/201207/ enjoy-trendsetter-natalie-coughlin-215.aspx.

60. Natalie Coughlin. "Summer Garden 2010." Facebook, Natalie Coughlin, July 14, 2010. www.facebook.com/ officialnataliecoughlin.

61. Quoted in Andrews. "Trendsetter."

62. Quoted in Camilla Samuels. "Natalie Coughlin: An Olympian Who Loves Food as Much as We Do." Yum Sugar, July 31, 2012. www.yumsugar.com/Natalie-Coughlin-Interview-About-Food-22813150.

63. Quoted in John Maher. "Coughlin Ready for the Bridge to London." *Austin American-Statesman*, March 4, 2010.

64. Quoted in Vicki Michaelis. "Coughlin Prefers to See the Little Picture as Historic Milestone Looms." *USA Today*, August 19, 2010. http://usatoday30.usatoday.com/printedition/ sports/20100819/olyswim19_st.art.htm.

65. Quoted in Rachel Tobin. "Dancing with the Stars: Natalie Coughlin Does Not Feel Good." Examiner.com, October 23, 2009. http://www.examiner.com/article/dancing-with-the-stars-natalie-coughlin-doesn-t-feel-good.

66. Natalie Couglin. Interview by Jay Leno. *The Tonight Show with Jay Leno*, season 19, episode 28. NBC, April 26, 2012. *The Tonight Show with Jay Leno*, NBC.com, http://www.nbc. com/the-tonight-show/video/olympic-swimmer-natalie-coughlin-part-1-42612/1398680/T.67.

67. Quoted in Kelsey Harkness. "Olympic Swimmer Natalie Coughlin on Retiring, Cookbooks and Body Paint." Fox News, September 20, 2012. http://magazine.foxnews.com/

food-wellness/olympic-swimmer-natalie-coughlin-retiring-cookbooks-and-body-paint.

68. Quoted in Eric Ball. "Natalie Coughlin: Body Paint Pictures Proof That Natural Beauty Still Trumps All." Bleacher Report, February 14, 2012. http://bleacherreport.com/articles/1066242-natalie-coughlin-body-paint-pictures-proof-that-natural-beauty-still-trumps-all.

69. Quoted in Michaelis. "Coughlin Prefers to See the Little Picture as Historic Milestone Looms."

70. Coughlin. *The Tonight Show with Jay Leno*.

71. Quoted in Rachel Blount. "Coughlin Ekes Way to 100 Freestyle Final." *Star Tribune*, June 30, 2012. http://www.startribune.com/sports/160922445.html.

72. Quoted in Blount. "Coughlin Ekes Way to 100 Freestyle Final."

73. Quoted in Bonnie D. Ford. "Natalie Coughlin Ready for Another Games." ESPN.com, June 30, 2012. http://espn.go.com/blog/olympics/post/_/id/2818/natalie-coughlin-ready-for-another-games.

74. Coughlin. *The Tonight Show with Jay Leno*.

# Important Dates

**1982**

Natalie Coughlin is born on August 23, 1982 in Vallejo, California, to Zennie and Jim Coughlin.

**1994**

Coughlin joins the Terrapin swim club.

**1998**

*Swimming World* magazine names Coughlin the National High School Swimmer of the Year.

**1999**

Coughlin injures her left shoulder.

**2000**

Coughlin graduates from high school; she meets Coach Teri McKeever and enters the University of California, Berkeley.

**2001**

Coughlin is named NCAA Swimmer of the Year.

**2002**

Coughlin is the first person since Tracy Caulkins in 1978 to win five national titles at one meet; she is named NCAA Swimmer of the Year and USA Swimming Swimmer of the Year.

**2003**

Coughlin is named NCAA Swimmer of the Year.

**2004**

Coughlin becomes a professional swimmer and the most decorated female athlete at the Olympics, winning five medals.

## 2005

Coughlin graduates from Berkeley with a degree in psychology.

## 2006

Coughlin is an Olympic analyst for MSNBC during the Winter Olympics; she writes an autobiography with Michael Silver.

## 2008

Coughlin becomes the first American woman in any sport to win six Olympic medals; she is named the United States Olympic Committee Sports Woman of the Year.

## 2009

Coughlin marries Ethan Hall; she becomes the spokesperson for the California Dried Plums Board and competes on *Dancing with the Stars*.

## 2012

Coughlin poses for *Sports Illustrated Swimsuit Edition*; she earns her twelfth Olympic medal, tying with Dara Torres and Jenny Thompson as the most decorated American female Olympian in history.

## Books

Matt Christopher. *Great Moments in the Summer Olympics*. New York: Little, Brown, 2012. This book is full of interesting facts about the Olympics, the history of the games, and the Olympic athletes and their struggles and triumphs.

Lizabeth Hardman. *Science Behind Sports: Swimming*. Farmington Hills, MI: Lucent Books, 2012. This book explores the physics, biology, health issues, psychology, and physiology involved in swimming.

Sue Macy. *Swifter, Higher, Stronger: A Photographic History of the Summer Olympics*. Washington, DC: National Geographic, 2008. This book presents a broad history of the summer Olympics with photos, a look at great Olympic athletes, and an almanac of quick facts.

Michael Silver. *Golden Girl*. With Natalie Coughlin. Emmaus, PA: Rodale, 2006. Coughlin's autobiography, written with the help of sports journalist Michael Silver, covers her life through 2004.

## Periodicals

Kelli Anderson. "The Next Golden Girl." *Sports Illustrated*, July 28, 2003. http://sportsillustrated.cnn.com/vault/article/magazine/MAG1029211/index/index.htm.

Cynthia Gorney. "A Feel for the Water." *New Yorker*, July 5, 2004.

Kayla Hutzler. "Olympic Swimmer Natalie Coughlin." *Muscle and Fitness/Hers*, July–August 2012.

Patricia Marx. "Natalie Coughlin Swimmer." *Vogue*, July 2004.

David Leon Moore. "Veteran Coughlin Prepares for Changing of the Guard." *USA Today*, July 27, 2012.

Gary Shelton. "A Legacy Immune to Age." *Tampa Bay Times*, June 30, 2012.

# Websites

**California Dried Plums** (www.californiadriedplums.org). This is the website of the California Dried Plum Board, an organization that protects and supports the dried plum industry in California. Coughlin is a spokesperson for California Dried Plum Board and its site offers some of her recipes and cooking videos as well as a short biography about her.

**Natalie Coughlin** (www.nataliecoughlin.com). This is Natalie Coughlin's official website. It contains photos and news about Coughlin.

**Facebook** (http://www.facebook.com/officialnataliecoughlin). Natalie Coughlin has an official page on Facebook that includes news about her daily life and lots of photos she has taken.

**Twitter** (https://twitter.com/NatalieCoughlin). Natalie Coughlin tweets about her life on this social media site.

A
Athens Olympics, 49, *53*, 53–54

B
Barcelona, World
  Championships in, 40, *41*, 42
Bauerle, Jack, 8
Beard, Amanda, 66
Beijing Olympics, 64–66, *67*, 68
Benicia Blue Dolphins, 13–14
Bennett, Steve, 16–17
Biography, 59, *60*, 61–62
Body painting, 75–76
Book, 59, *60*, 61–62
Bootsma, Rachel, 79
Bruijn, Inge de, 51

C
California Dried Plum Board, 72
Careers, sports-related, 63
Carondelet High School, 19
Charities, 63–64
Chickens, raising, 72
Childhood
  activities, 14
  first swim team, 13–14
  school, 15
Children, role modeling for,
  62–64
Coaches
  Bennett, Steve, 16–17
  McKeever, Teri, 29–33
  Quick, Richard, 27, 29
  Williams, Tuffy, 13
College
  academics, 33–34

choosing, 26–27, 29
  graduation, 57
  hobbies and social life, 34
Competitiveness, *10*, 10–11, 14,
  16–17
Cooking, 34, 37, 57–59, *58*
Cope, Haley, 34, 44, *50*, 51
Coughlin, Jim, 21
Coughlin, Jim and Zennie, *15*
  Benicia Blue Dolphins, 13
  childhood activities, 14
  college choice, 26–27, 29
  Terrapins, 17
Coughlin, Megan, 15, *15*, 34
Coventry, Kristy, 66

D
*Dancing with the Stars* (television
  show), 9, 73–75, *74*
Diet, 58–59, 72
Disqualification in first meet, 14
Douglas, Gabby, 76

E
Edible Schoolyard program, 72
Elementary school, 15
Endorsement deals, 47–48
Ethnicity, 16
Evangelista, Mila, 15
Evans, Janet, 29

F
Female on Campus Athlete of
  the Year, *Sports Illustrated,* 37
Filipino roots, 16
Flexibility, 11

Franklin, Missy, 8, 76, 79
Friends and social life, 19, 21, 34
Future plans, 81

G
Gaines, Rowdy, 37
Gair, Joanne, 75
Gardening, 70–71, *71*
Guthrie, Savannah, *58*

H
Hall, Ethan, 21, 23, 24, 34, 51,
  69–70
High school, *18*, 18–19
Hobbies
  chickens, raising, 72
  college life, 34
  cooking, 57–59
  gardening, 70–71
  physical activities, 14
  variety of, 8–9

I
Illnesses, 9, 40, 42
Inaba, Carrie Ann, 74
Injuries, 9, 21–25, 30–31, 57

L
Lafayette, CA, 70–71
Language, 16
Leno, Jay, 75, 78
Let's Move campaign, 72–73
London Olympics, 76, 78–80, *79*
Long-distance swimming, 17

M
Marriage, 69–70
Mazo, Alec, 74, *74*
McKeever, Teri, *30*
  coaching style, 29–33
  Coughlin-team relations, 44

Olympic training, 49
Olympics, 2004, 49, 51
Olympics, 2012, 80–81
Media
  Olympics, promotion of the,
    *49*, 52
  post-2004 Olympics appear-
    ances, 55
  public appearances, 55, *56*
Middle-distance swimming, 17
Miller, Janey, 46–47
Miller, Marcelle, 44
Mitchell, Ray, 17–19,
  21–25, 61
Monroe, Leah, 19
Morales, Natalie, *58*
Motivation, 33
MSNBC, 62

N
National Championships, 18
National High School Swimmer
  of the Year (*Swimming
  World*), 19
National titles, 35
NCAA
  records set, 35, 37, 39
  Swimmer of the Year honors,
    27, 35
  winning streak, 48–49
Nelms, Mike, 31
Nike, 47–48

O
Oakland A's game, 45, *46*
Obama, Michelle, 72–73, *73*
Octagon Agency, 45
Olympic trials
  2000, 22, 24–25
  2004, *50*
  2008, *65*

Olympics
  history, 52
  records set, 8
  torch carrying, 66
  2004, 49, 53, 53–54
  2006, 62
  2008, 64–66, 67, 68
  2012, 76, 78–80, 79
  2016, 81
100-meter freestyle, 51

P
Personality
  competitiveness, 10–11, 14,
    16–17
  motivation, 33
  personality clash with coach
    Ray Mitchell, 21
Phelps, Michael, 45
Photography, 57
Physical attributes, 11
Physical therapy, 22–23
Professional status, 37, 39
Psychology major, 33
Public appearances, 55, *56*
Public image, 45, *46*

Q
Quick, Richard, 27, 29

R
Richards-Ross, Sanya, 76
Right To Play, 63–64
Roker, Al, 37, *58*
Role modeling, 62–64

S
Sanders, Summer, 29
School, 15
Shoulder injury, 21–25, 30–31
Silver, Michael, 59, 62

Speedo, 47–48
Sports agents, 45–47
Sports broadcasting, 9, 62
*Sports Illustrated* (magazine)
  Female on Campus Athlete of
    the Year, 37
  *Swimsuit Edition,* 75–76
Sports Woman of the Year,
    United States Olympic
    Committee, 69
Springs, 35
Stanford University, 26–27,
    29, 39
Strokes, swimming, 17, 31–32
Summer Olympics, 52
Swimmer of the Year, NCAA,
    35, 37
Swimmer of the Year, USA
    Swimming, 37
Swimming
  physics of, 68
  strokes, 17, 31–32
  tapering, 80
  terminology, 36
  trivia, 47
  underwater duration, 11–12
*Swimming World* (magazine), 19

T
Tagalog, 16
Tapering, 80
Television
  appearances, 9, 37, 55
  *Dancing with the Stars,* 73–75
  sports broadcasting, 62
  *Today* appearance, *58*
Terminology, 36
Terrapins swim team, 17, 19, *20*,
    21–25, 61
Thompson, Jenny, 8, 29, 81
*Today* (television show), 37, *58*

Torres, Dara, 8, 66, 81
Training
  book revelations, 59, 61
  dedication to, 11
  McKeever, Teri, coaching style
    of, 29–33
  Mitchell, Ray, coaching style of,
    17, 19, 21–25
  Olympic trials, 2004, 49–51
  tapering, 80

U
Underwater duration, 11–12
United States Olympic
  Committee, 69
University of California,
  Berkeley, *28, 32, 35, 38, 43*
  choosing, 26–27, 29

spokesperson position, 37
teammates, relationship with,
  42, 44
USA Swimming, 37

V
Vallejo, California, 16

W
Walker, Mike, 29
Waters, Alice, 72
Williams, Tuffy, 13
Winning streak, 48–49
World Championships
  record for medals, 8
  2003, 9, 40, *41*, 42
  2011, *77*, 78
World records, 35, 37, 64

# Picture Credits

# About the Author

Barbara Sheen is the author of more than seventy books for young people. She lives in New Mexico with her family. Like Natalie Coughlin, she loves to swim and cook.

# WITHDRAWN